Piero Torriti

former Superintendent of Artistic and Historical Assets
for the Provinces of Siena and Grosseto

Siena

History and Masterpieces

BONECHI
edizioni il Turismo
FIRENZE - 1954

© Copyright by Bonechi - Edizioni "Il Turismo" S.r.l.
Via dei Rustici, 5 - 50122 Firenze
Tel. +39-055.239.82.24/25
Fax +39-055.21.63.66
E-mail: barbara@bonechi.com
E-mail: bbonechi@dada.it
http://www.bonechi.com

Publishing editor: Barbara Bonechi
Graphics and layout: Paola Rufino
Editing and iconographic research: Lorena Lazzari
Photos: – Archives of Bonechi Edizioni "Il Turismo" S.r.l.,
            by Nicola Grifoni - Florence
          – Foto 3 by Lensini Fabio e C.S.n.c.- Siena
The photos on pages 27, 28, 29 are of works in the Chigi Saracini
Collection - Property of the Banca Monte dei Paschi di Siena S.p.A.
The photos on pages 5 (below), 8 (below), 104 (below, right), 105, 106,
107 are works owned by the Banca Monte dei Paschi di Siena S.p.A.
Photo page 102 (below): Enoteca Italica - Siena
Photo pages 115, 116: Courtesy of the Ministry for Cultural Assets
and Affairs – State Archives of Siena
Drawing on page 7 from: A. Cairola - E. Carli "Il Palazzo Pubblico
di Siena", Rome 1963
Drawing on page 34 from: "La Ricerca delle origini", OPA, 1998
Photolithography: Bluprint Srl., Florence
Printed: BO.BA.DO.MA., Florence
ISBN: 88-7204-475-8

* *This book presents the locations of the artworks at the time
  of printing.*

* *Everything possible has been done to ascertain the legitimate
  owners of the rights for individual illustrations. In case there have
  been any involuntary omissions, we will be happy to pay the user fees.*

Siena was founded by the Romans during the reign of Octavian Augustus. They built a military colony (Saena Julia) on the site of a preexisting Etruscan and perhaps Gallic (the Saenones) settlement. The Roman origins of the town explain the heraldic charge the Medieval town chose for itself (the she-wolf feeding Romulus and Remus), which, together with the argent and sable coat divided per fess (la Balzana) were used by the town as its arms. Roman Siena was never very important, chiefly because it did not lie on any of the main consular roads (Aurelia and Cassia), which originally wound along the coast and through the Chiana Valley. For the same reasons, Christianity only reached Sienese territory towards the beginning of the 4th century. After the first Barbarian invasions had swept through Italy and after the Byzantine-Gothic war, Siena became part of the Lombard dominions. The Lombards settled in Siena and promoted the expansion of the Sienese territory to the detriment of nearby Arezzo. The road network shifted its axis and the Aurelia and the Cassia, which passed through areas exposed to the Byzantine raids, were gradually abandoned in favor of the Via Francigena, that linked the Northern Lombard possessions with Rome, passing through Siena. In 774, the Lombards surrendered to Charlemagne and Siena was overrun by Frankish administrators, who married into the Lombard families, originating the oldest aristocratic families in Siena and founding abbeys and castles all over the Sienese territory. Feudal power gradually decreased and at the death of the Countess Matilda (1115), the Mark of Tuscia, which under the Canossa family (Matilda's) included most of Tuscany as it is today, broke up into a series of fledgling communal structures. The Commune of Siena, with its territory bordering dangerously on Guelph Florence, a traditional enemy of Siena, declared its allegiance to the Ghibelline cause. Between the 12th and 13th centuries, the early-Medieval «civitas» of Siena expanded, joining the two boroughs or agglomerations of houses that had grown up along the Via Franci-

▼ *A bird's eye view of Siena.*

gena, to the north and east of the town, thus originating the three districts, *terzi*, of Città, Camollia and San Martino. Money-lending and exchange activities brought the city great prosperity, the business expanded all over Europe (Champagne, Flanders and England) and under the Buonsignori created the largest European banking company in the 13th century. The large Sienese hospital of S. Maria della Scala that had been founded by the cathedral canons prior to the year one thousand also gained in importance during this period, and the office of the Biccherna (the financial magistrature) and the General Council became stronger as well. Towards the beginning of the 13th century, the consular regime was replaced by the Podestà system and Siena became one of the most active Tuscan partisans of Frederick II's successor, Manfred of Swabia, King of Sicily. The war against Florence reached its apex at the battle of Montaperti, when the Sienese army massacred the Guelph army of Florence (4 September 1260). The regime of the Podestàs fell in Siena as it did in the Northern and Central Italian towns, when the burgher class started demanding that it should share the administrative power in the town together with the patricians. The regime of the Nine commenced in 1287 and lasted for many tranquil years. Its representatives were mostly rich burghers who were appointed in rotation every two months. This was the period during which the Salimbeni, Tolomei, Sansedoni, Buonsignori, Piccolomini and Gallerani families rose to power and countless great artists such as Duccio di Buoninsegna, Simone Martini, Ambrogio and Piero Lorenzetti, Nicola and Giovanni Pisano, Tino da Camaino and many others graced Siena with their presence. These were the years when the construction of the Palazzo Pubblico was commenced, when the plans for enlarging the Cathedral (never completed) were drawn, when the last circle of the walls (still standing) was built. In 1348, Siena, like most of Europe, was hit by the terrible Black Death, which not only exterminated four-fifths of the population, but destabilized the political scene. When the Government of the Nine was overthrown in 1355, the "Monti" or groups of powerful patrician and burgher families took over the government. Caterina Benincasa (St. Catherine of Siena), a typical exponent of medieval religious Siena, lived during this period, and Bartolo di Fredi, Taddeo di Bartolo, Andrea di Bartolo, etc. emerged on the painting scene. During the 1390's, in order to protect herself from Florence, Siena placed herself under the Seigneury of Gian Galeazzo Visconti, Duke of Milan, but after his death (1404), the turbulent, communal strife resumed. These were the years in which the great Sienese painters flourished such as Sassetta, Vecchietta, Francesco di Giorgio Martini, and Sano di Pietro. The outstanding sculptor of the period was Jacopo della Quercia, while the humanist pope Pius II (Enea Silvio Piccolomini)

▼ *The Mangia Tower.*

▲ *Detail of a fresco by Sano di Pietro*
(Palazzo Pubblico, Sala delle Lupe).

promoted the activity on Sienese soil of Florentine artists like Bernardo Rossellino. At the end of the fifteenth century Siena had to accept the alliance with Charles V of Spain, who ordered a fortress built for the Spanish forces within the town, arousing violent popular reaction that led to the break-up of the alliance (1552) with the Emperor of Spain, who then sought the support of Cosimo I de' Medici in Florence. Siena became an ally of France, but in the end, beleaguered by the Florentine and Spanish forces, was forced to capitulate in April 1555. Siena was handed over to Philip II, King of Spain, who granted it in fief to Cosimo I de' Medici (who thus became Duke of Florence and Siena and subsequently, in 1569, Grand Duke of Tuscany, thanks to the extension of the territories under his power). Under the Medici family, Siena clung to the memory of her former freedom and the factious spirit of her inhabitants, no longer allowed to participate in the political life of the city, was unleashed in passionate allegiance to the respective «contrade» of each native of Siena. The city maintained its independence in the artistic field, thanks to Domenico Beccafumi, Baldassarre Peruzzi and others. The banking tradition evolved from the private to the public status and the ancient Monte di Pietà founded in 1472 became the Monte dei Paschi in 1624. After the advent of the Hapsburg-Lorraine family (1737), the last vestiges of the Republic disappeared and the city became an integral part of the Grand Duchy of Tuscany. The city's marked spiritual individuality is however apparent today in the attachment each Sienese feels towards his or her contrada and in the passionate involvement in the Palio, the most evident example of the exuberant nature of Siena's citizens.

▼ *Procession of the Contrade,*
by Vincenzo Rustici
(Collection of the Monte dei Paschi di Siena).

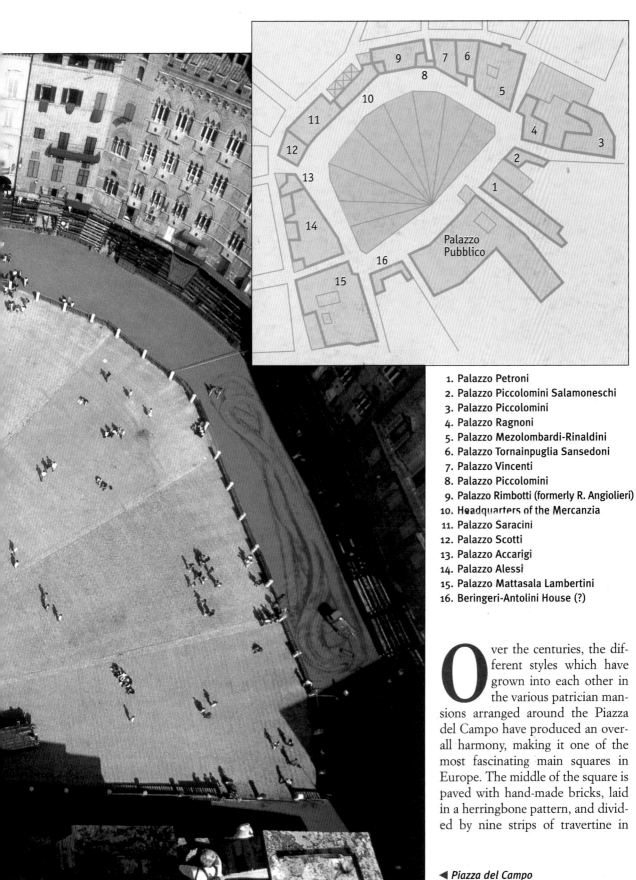

1. Palazzo Petroni
2. Palazzo Piccolomini Salamoneschi
3. Palazzo Piccolomini
4. Palazzo Ragnoni
5. Palazzo Mezolombardi-Rinaldini
6. Palazzo Tornainpuglia Sansedoni
7. Palazzo Vincenti
8. Palazzo Piccolomini
9. Palazzo Rimbotti (formerly R. Angiolieri)
10. Headquarters of the Mercanzia
11. Palazzo Saracini
12. Palazzo Scotti
13. Palazzo Accarigi
14. Palazzo Alessi
15. Palazzo Mattasala Lambertini
16. Beringeri-Antolini House (?)

Over the centuries, the different styles which have grown into each other in the various patrician mansions arranged around the Piazza del Campo have produced an overall harmony, making it one of the most fascinating main squares in Europe. The middle of the square is paved with hand-made bricks, laid in a herringbone pattern, and divided by nine strips of travertine in

◀ *Piazza del Campo*
from the Mangia Tower.

▲ *Piazza del Campo.*

cepted by that intense spirit of republican freedom that is still an example for today's democracies. Of all the events in the square, most important was and still is the Palio horse race. It is held here every year on 2 July and on 16 August. It is impossible to speak of the history of Siena and her people without mentioning the "contrade" and the Palio. The race is not a mere popular tradition or folkloristic event, but a true synthesis of an ancient custom of a people who, throughout the year, in every important public or private act or deed relives and merges past and present in a remarkable continuity, as in a small but real democratic republic.

honor of the Government of the Nine Lords (i Signori Nove) that presided over the town from 1285 to 1355. Nearly all the important events in Siena's history have taken place in or around this square. Some of them were auspicious, others less so; some took place during the glorious era of the Republic (before 1555), others after the city became a dominion of Florence. This period of domination was never fully ac-

▼ *View of Piazza del Campo,*
by Giuseppe Zocchi
(Collection of the Monte dei Paschi di Siena).

FONTE GAIA

In order to channel water from distant Staggia to Piazza del Campo, Giacomo di Vanni di Ugolino (later called Giacomo dell'Acqua) spent about eight years digging great underground canals (which are still known as the Bottini) which, as they approached the town precincts, widened into brick-lined galleries of exceptional technical and artistic interest. Charles V, after visiting the Sienese "bottini", is supposed to have exclaimed that Siena was two cities in one, each as beautiful as the other, the first underground, the second above. Water was conveyed to Piazza del Campo through a master-conduit, most likely first utilized around 1342. "The Sienese saluted the event with great rejoicing", wherefore the fountain,

▲ Interior of the master conduit (bottino) of the Fonte Gaia.

▼ The Fonte Gaia, by Jacopo della Quercia, before its removal from Piazza del Campo, in a nineteenth century photo.

▲ Tito Sarrocchi's adaptation of the Fonte Gaia.

appropriately named Fonte Gaia (Joyous Fountain), was built the following year (1343). The 14th century Fonte Gaia, about which we have practically no information, was replaced in 1419 by Jacopo della Quercia's and then by Tito Sarrocchi's free adaptation of it in 1858. The two statues of Rhea Silvia and Acca Larentis, that Jacopo had placed at each end of his fountain, were omitted from Sarrocchi's copy. The original sculptures by Jacopo della Quercia are now in a room in the old Ospedale di S. Maria della Scala that overlooks Piazza Duomo. Although its present state is decidedly lamentable, Jacopo's Fonte Gaia is still one of the most important sculptures produced in 15th century

▲ Detail of the Fonte Gaia today.

◄ *Rhea Silvia,*
by Jacopo della Quercia
(Ospedale di S. Maria
della Scala).

Italy during the transition from the Gothic to the Renaissance styles. The *Madonna and Child*, a symbol taken from Lorenzetti's Allegory of Good Government, is flanked by two angels, the *Theological* and *Cardinal Virtues* and by *Justice*. Successive changes in the project led Jacopo to add the reliefs with the *Expulsion from Paradise*, the *Creation of Adam* as well as the two statues of *Acca Larentis* and *Rhea Silvia* (respectively mother and nurse of Romulus and Remus, symbolizing Charity and Liberality). These were the first two statues of female nudes to stand in a public place, who were neither Eve nor a repentant saint.

◄ *Detail with the Expulsion*
from Paradise, by Jacopo
della Quercia (Ospedale
di S. Maria della Scala).

Because of a solemn vow made during the terrible plague of 1348, the Commune of Siena commissioned the Cappella di Piazza which stands out at the foot of the Mangia Tower. At first, Domenico di Agostino, then master builder at the Opera del Duomo (Cathedral Works) and brother to the better known Giovanni, was put in charge of the project. The four corner piers, called "more", were built somewhat later, in 1376, by Giovanni di Cecco. A plain roof covered the piers until Antonio Federighi replaced it during the Renaissance (1461-1468) with a vaulted roof, supported by rounded arches, with niches in the corners, garlands adorning the pendentives and a purely classical architrave decorated with a frieze of gryphons and vases. The side balustrades are two 13th century marble panels, which are thought to have come from the ancient Baptismal Font in the Cathedral. The two figures of Arithmetic and Geometry, on the front panels, were sculpted by Guidoccio Cozzarelli (1470). In 1848, they were replaced by copies carved by Enea Becheroni while the Cozzarelli originals were placed inside the Palace on the walls of the main staircase. The elegant grilles in wrought iron on either side of the Chapel were made in the second half of the 14th century. They probably belonged to the first Chapel of the Nine, on the ground floor of the Palazzo Pubblico, and were forged by Pietro di Betto, helped, according to some accounts, by Conte di Lello Orlandi, another Sienese master smith. To the left of the altar, behind a small, old wrought-iron grille, there is a stone shrine, with an *Annunciation* and a *Christ Blessing* on the tympanum, by an unknown Sienese carver of the late 14th century. The figures are reminiscent of Goro di Gregorio's style. The fresco above the altar, with the *Madonna and Child, Angels and the Almighty*, is almost indecipherable. It was painted by Sodoma between 1537 and 1539.

▼ *Chapel of Piazza del Campo.*

PALAZZO PUBBLICO

It is thought that the first nucleus was a low, one-story construction with a simple stone façade, and four openings leading into a large hall and a courtyard, that was finished around 1284 as related by the chronicles of Paolo Tommaso Montauri that year. In 1288, however, the Council decided to construct a new palace at the bottom of the Campo. A few years later, the construction of the central part of the palace was commenced.

It was not unlike the building we see today: the stone-dressed ground-floor with its four ogival openings; the first brick story with four triple mullioned windows and the second story, also in brick, which probably had five triple mullioned windows to start with, later reduced to four, for the sake of uniformity, while the two second floor wings were added in 1680, in the Baroque period. The building was probably finished around 1310, as the Government of the Nine adopted it as their headquarters in that year. The nine members of the government were never allowed out of the palace except on Feast days. The ground-floor façade had ten open doorways, of which the fourth from the right of anyone looking at the building, led into the Chapel of the Nine, frescoed by 14th century painters. After the fairly drastic restoration carried out during the late 1890s and the early 1900s, the façade has taken on a plain, fairly undecorated appearance. The architectural elements soar vertically upwards, only interrupted by the large double and triple mullioned windows and countering all sense of massive strength with the frail elegance of the façade's delicate linearism. The Siena *arms* or *Balzana* are set into the ogival arch of each window, whilst the great *Plaque of St. Bernardino* (the monogram of Christ, IHS, surrounded by rays) replaces the original central twin mullioned window on the third story level. The *Medici arms* were added in 1560 to commemorate the annexation of Siena to the Grand Duchy of Tuscany. The Medici crest is flanked by the *Balzana* and by the people's *Lion Rampant*. Two stone *she-wolf* gargoyles protrude on each side of the central block. The main entrance tympanum has the *Lion of the people* in the center, flanked by two she-wolves in relief while a statuette of *St. Ansanus* stands above the tympanum. At the end of the façade, near the main entrance, there used to be a granite column bearing the gilded bronze *she-wolf with the Roman twins*, cast by Giovanni and Lorenzo di Turino in 1430. This beautiful group has now been placed inside the palace in order to preserve it. The she-wolf suckling Romulus and Remus is the symbol of Siena. The mythical brothers, Aschius and Senius, sons of Remus, are supposed to have fled

▼ *The Palazzo Pubblico in a 19th century engraving.*

▲ *The Palazzo Pubblico.*

▲ *The Courtyard of the Podestà.*

from the wrath of Romulus, bearing an effigy of the Roman she-wolf, as a symbol of their lost homeland, with them. They reputedly took refuge in the Tuscan hills, where Senius later founded the city (Senius/ Sena/Siena).

The **Mangia Tower**, which gets its name from Giovanni di Balduccio or Duccio, nicknamed Mangiaguadagni (literally earnings-gobbler) or Mangia (Gobbler), who used to be the bell-ringer before a mechanism was installed to replace him, lends the whole complex of the Palazzo Pubblico its extraordinarily delicate, vertical elegance. It was started in 1325 and finished in 1348. It was intended as a symbol of the power residing in the palace and of the city itself. The tower is 87 m. high (102 m., if we include the lightning rod). The brothers Francesco and Muccio (or Minuccio) di Rinaldo from Arezzo were commissioned to do the construction work (1338-40) and they therefore shouldered the risks and expense of the building operations The tower is entirely in brick, up to the soaring white travertine pronged supports of the belfry balustrade, which give the whole tower the appearance of a tall slender lily. The latter part was probably built by Agostino di Giovanni, based on the designs of a certain "Master Lippo-painter", almost certainly the great Lippo Memmi, brother-in-law to Simone Martini (1341). The present master bell (called "Campanone", or "Sunto")

weighs 6764 kgs. and was hung in the belfry in 1666.

There are at present two entries to the Town Hall on the Piazza. The first, through the two doors to the left, next to the Chapel, leads into the **Courtyard of the Podestà** where, amidst the many *family crests* of the governors, the remains of the

◄ *The Mangia Tower.*

◄ *The She-wolf, by Giovanni di Turino.*

▲ *The Battle of S. Martino, by Amos Cassioli (Room of the Risorgimento).*

The other door, on the right, opens onto a corridor, leading to a steep staircase which climbs up to the Loggia and the upper floors. Beyond the corridor one enters the **Sala di Balia** (Hall of the Aldermen), where the Bailie (the representatives of the executive power of the Republic, generally eight citizens, with extensive powers), met from 1455 on. The hall is completely frescoed in Late Gothic style by a Sienese (Martino di Bartolomeo) and by a

▼ *The Sala di Balia (Hall of the Aldermen), with frescoes by Spinello Aretino.*

stone *statue of Mangia* are preserved. At the end of the courtyard, steps lead up to the **Teatro dei Rinnovati**, formerly the Great Council Chamber of the Republic. A side door opens onto a modern staircase leading down to a whole series of lovely, semi-underground halls, with brick vaults, once the cisterns and storerooms of the Palace ("**Magazzini del Sale**" or "Salt Storerooms"), which have been beautifully restored and are now used for temporary exhibitions. The same staircase leads to the piano nobile and the rooms containing the **Quadreria** or Picture Gallery of various schools and periods, mostly moved here from the old Civic Museum. The next room is the **Room of the Risorgimento** (the former Audience Room of the Podestà) where a large number of 19th century sculptures have been arranged. The Room of the Risorgimento, however, is known for the scenes on the walls, by 19th century Tuscan artists, recounting episodes from the life of Vittorio Emanuele II.

▲ *Wood inlay, by Mattia di Nanni known as Bernacchino.*

well as six *busts of emperors and warriors*, including, they say, Godfrey of Bouillon, on the piers and pendentives of the arch itself. In 1408, Spinello Aretino was given the more complicated task of recording the *deeds of Pope Alexander III*, a member of the Sienese Bandinelli family, the inspiring force behind the Lombard League and deadly enemy of Barbarossa (Frederick Redbeard) as well as probable promoter of the foundation of the Cathedral of Siena.

The beautiful inlaid *door*, (1426) which leads into the **Inner Chapel**, is attributed to Domenico di Niccolò (called «dei Cori» because he also made the wonderful carved and inlaid *choir stalls* of the palace chapel). The magnificent choir flanking the altar was carved by Domenico di Niccolò between 1514

citizen of Arezzo, who had learned his craft in Florence, Spinello Aretino, named after his hometown Arezzo. The former painted the *Virtues* on the vault sections and on the pillars and the *four Evangelists* on the intrados of the great arch that divides the hall into two, as

▼ *The Inner Chapel with frescoes by Taddeo di Bartolo.*

▲ *The Funeral of the Virgin Mary, by Taddeo di Bartolo.*

(1414) in the **Antechapel**; the cycle quite obviously refers to the ideas and lifestyle of the Sienese republic in the early 15th century. There are five *Virtues* illustrated (*Fortitude, Prudence, Faith, Justice* and *Magnanimity*), surrounded by the portraits of illustrious personalities of ancient Rome (*Cato, Brutus, Mutius Scaevola, Attilius Regulus, Scipio*, etc.). The intrados of the great arch, on the Sala del Mappamondo (Map Room) side, is decorated with a *view of Rome*, surrounded by the figures of *Jupiter, Mars, Apollo, Pallas Athena, Aristotle, Caesar* and *Pompey*. In 1959, the gilded bronze she-wolf feeding the twins was

▼ *The Holy Family, by Sodoma.*

and 1428. There are 21 stalls each decorated with a scene illustrating *some article of the Creed*. Also by Domenico, the splendid left door frame decorated with a Nativity scene and a *Wheel*, symbolizing the allegories of good and bad power. The vaults and walls of the chapel were all frescoed by the late-Gothic Sienese painter, Taddeo di Bartolo, with five *Scenes from the Life of the Virgin*. On the altar there is painting by Antonio Bazzi known as Sodoma, portraying the *Holy Family* and *St. Leonard*; this is one of the most significant paintings by the artist from Vercelli who belonged to Leonardo's school (1530-35). There is a carved and gilded wooden *chandelier* hanging from the vault of the chapel; it had incorrectly been attributed to Cecco di Nanni del Ciucca and painted by Cristofano da Cosona. It has more recently been recognized as having been carved by Domenico di Niccolò dei Cori shortly before 1435. Taddeo di Bartolo also painted the colossal *St. Christopher* (1408) and a cycle of political Virtues and illustrious men placed in the vestibule. The statue was cast in 1429 by Giovanni di Turino and his son Lorenzo and was placed on the column in front of the Palazzo Pubblico.

Next to the chapel is the great hall, called **Sala del Mappamondo** (Map Room), where the Council of the Republic met. The end wall is decorated by Simone Martini's magnificent **Maestà** (1315 and 1321), one of the greatest European Gothic masterpieces. The novel significant concepts this work expresses, compared for instance, with the

▼ *Maestà, by Simone Martini* (Sala del Mappamondo).

▲ *Detail of the Maestà, by Simone Martini.*

other famous *Maestà* by Duccio di Buoninsegna in the Museo dell'Opera del Duomo (Cathedral Museum), are a perfect definition of the new ideals of the 14th century, which blossom in the pages of Petrarch's *Canzoniere* (Petrarch was a friend of Simone) or in Boccacio's

▲ *Sala del Mappamondo (Map Room).*

▲ *The wall with Guidoriccio in the Sala del Mappamondo. In the upper part, the Siege of Montemassi, by Simone Martini; at the center, the Surrender of a Castle (Giuncarico?), by Duccio di Buoninsegna; at the sides, Saints Ansanus and Victor, by Sodoma.*

Decameron. Simone's frescoed Virgin no longer conforms to the strict canons of Byzantine iconography, as Duccio's Madonna does in his gigantic panel. She is a more human «Mater», who has graciously descended amidst the people of Siena, while two angels offer bowls brimming with flowers, as she sits among her heavenly retinue. These were new emotions compared with the early Middle Ages. It is the compositional aspect that is more revolutionary than the figures and the subject, with harmonious lines flowing almost uninterruptedly from one figure to the other, and soft, transparent colors. The upper part of the end wall opposite the Maestà is frescoed with the *1328 Siege of the Castle of Montemassi in Maremma led by Guidoriccio da Fogliano*, then captain of the Sienese army. Simone Martini's name is also linked to this world-famous fresco that has become the symbol of the civilian and military glory of the ancient Republic of Siena and is a kind of contrast to the religious glory epitomized by the courtly language used in the

▲ *The Surrender of a Castle (Giuncarico?), attributed to Duccio da Buoninsegna.*

Maestà on the opposite wall. The knight in his tunic embroidered with the device of the Da Fogliano family (twining vines sprouting from a line of dark blue lozenges on golden ground) rides a horse caparisoned with the same device. Although the features of the knight are portrayed with due attention, the central group appears to possess no physical solidity whatsoever, as if the modulated construction were an abstract symphony of pure musical chords, repeated in the flowing line of lozenges on the caparisoned horse and on the knight's tunic, the whole offset by the unstable equilibrium of the horse, that seems to be floating in mid-air. This unreal metaphysical quality enhances the magic of the scene. Its apparition-like sense can also be perceived in the landscape, where the castle of Montemassi, the keep with its turrets and catapult and the Sienese army encampment stand out against the barren clay hills of the Maremma.

◄ *Siege of the Castle of Montemassi Led by Guidoriccio da Fogliano, by Simone Martini.*

▲ *The Room of Peace.*

ably be attributed to Duccio di Buoninsegna (1314-1315). Adjacent to the Map Room is the Room of the Nine, better known as the **Room of Peace**, thanks to an allegorical figure painted there. The frescoes, of great artistic and historic value, are world-famous. They cover three sides of the room and represent the *Allegory of Good and Bad Government*, which the great Ambrogio Lorenzetti was commissioned to paint for the Government of the Nine, between 1338 and 1340. On the short wall opposite the large windows is the Allegory of Good Government proper. It is rich in inscriptions identifying the various figures and centers on the old man, dressed in black and white (the colors of Siena) symbolizing both the city and the common weal; the she-wolf feeding the twins is at his feet. The old man is flanked by *Peace, Fortitude, Prudence, Magnanimity,*

During careful restorations in 1981, under the direction of this writer, yet another exceptional fresco was found below the Guidoriccio scene. It is certainly older and depicts the *peaceful surrender of a castle* (Giuncarico in Maremma) to the Sienese. This fresco can most prob-

▲ *Detail of Good Government, by Ambrogio Lorenzetti* (Room of Peace).

add a note of deeper humanity to the magnificent composition. The ethical and political meanings which Simone Martini expressed in a totally different vein in the frescoes we have just described in the Map Room, are reiterated in this Allegory by Ambrogio in a far more precise and less abstract fashion with the object of pointing out that a good government can only be based on the Virtues (with special reference to Justice and Concord) which spontaneously generate Safety, flying high above the red gate of Siena, in the fresco on the right wall.

Ambrogio's cycle (the first to be based on a secular theme in the his-

Temperance and *Justice*, with *Faith, Hope* and *Charity* above his head. Knights in armor stand guard, below right, over a group of prisoners or evil-doers. The slow procession of the rulers conversing among themselves winds its way towards him, while the knights and prisoners

▼ *Effects of Good Government in the City of Siena, by Ambrogio Lorenzetti* (Room of Peace).

▲ *Sala del Concistoro (Room of the Concistory), with frescoes by Beccafumi.*

ity) and he is flanked by the sinister figures of *Cruelty, Deceit, Fraudulence, Fury, Discord* and *War. Avarice, Pride* and *Vainglory* crowd around his head. The humiliated figure of Justice in chains crouches beneath the throne. After admiring other, minor works in the last room, we retrace our steps through the antechapel and enter the last room via an elegant Renaissance marble doorway, carved by Bernardo Rossellino in 1446, (the carved and inlaid doors were made by Domenico di Niccolò dei Cori in 1444). The hall is called **Sala del Concistoro** (Room of the Concistory), or Room of the Tapestries, because of the three magnificent Gobelin tapestries, woven to designs by Charles Le Brun (17th century) hanging on the walls. They represent the *Allegories of Earth, Air* and *Fire*. The fourth, with the Allegory of Water is still in the Uffizi gallery in Florence, where the three Sienese ones originally came from. The

tory of painting, as many art historians have observed) reaches its peak on the right wall, where he portrayed the *Effects of Good Government on Siena and its territory*. The delightfully realistic details of the happy, well-governed city, inhabited by its content, industrious citizens engaged in their manifold activities both within and outside the walls are depicted in all their variety beneath the winged figure of Safety hovering above the russet gate of Siena. This is the first painting in the history of art where timeless modernity is expressed without the mediation of symbolism: a happy life is depicted in the city and countryside, with shops open on the street, a school, processions, and children playing. The contentment of the farmers harvesting their crops, and the beautiful countryside are portrayed through masterful use of color. On the opposite wall,

much of the fresco of the effects of *Bad Government* has been destroyed over the years due to negligence. The allegory itself centers on the figure of *Tyranny* enthroned. At his feet is a black billy-goat (*Bestial-*

▼ *The Murder of Spurious Maelius, by Domenico Beccafumi (Sala del Concistoro).*

great artistic importance of this room is mainly due, however, to the superbly luminous frescoes that Domenico di Pace, called Beccafumi, painted between 1529 and 1535 on the ceiling vaults. Like Ambrogio Lorenzetti before him in the Room of Peace, he depicted episodes of *civic Virtue* drawn from Valerius Maximus. Beccafumi's brilliant colors create a feeling of crystalline purity and transparent delicacy and the clarity of the fresco's luminous tones, combined with the airy, beautifully executed perspective are in perfect accord with the most refined Tuscan Mannerist dictates, to such an extent that the technical and pictorial ability employed lend the whole a vaguely cold and artificial sensation. There is an admirable painting by Luca Giordano (Naples 1634-1705) of the *Judgement of Solomon* above the doorway. The robust chiaroscuro effects owe much to another Neapolitan painter Mattia Preti, but also reflect a resounding range of color effects drawn from the neo-Venetian school. It was probably painted around 1675-80, before Giordano left for Florence. Today, most of the offices of the city government are on the ground-floor of the palace and can be entered from Piazza del Campo via the second door on the right. Many of the ground floor rooms are also decorated with paintings and mainly frescoes, by more or less renowned artists starting from the 14th century, followers of Simone Martini, Bartolo di Fredi, Sano di Pietro, Vecchietta, Sodoma, Rutilio Manetti, and other 18th century Sienese painters.

In the 14th century, splendid family mansions, nearly all in brick with double or triple-mullioned windows surrounded the square, as a decree contained in the Statute of the Republic ordained. They were

◀ Beheading of Spurius Cassius Vecellinus, by Domenico Beccafumi (Sala del Concistoro).

separated by the narrow alleys leading into the square itself. The diagram on page 7 shows who owned each mansion in the Middle Ages. Even though most of these buildings were transformed or even entirely rebuilt, the original harmony of the Medieval square is still evident.

From Piazza del Campo, we must go up the *Costarella dei Barbieri* to reach the Cathedral. This is starting point and finish line for the Palio race. Opposite, on Via di Città, is the tower-house that used to be the seat of the Podestà (governor) of Siena, which leads on to the *neighboring Palazzo Pollini*, that stands between the left corner of the Costarella and the Via di Città, which at this point starts ascending slowly towards the old city center. *Via di Città*, formerly Via Galgaria, is one of the loveliest and most elegant streets in Siena. It is lined with buildings constructed in various periods, starting from the 13th century, when many wooden houses were replaced by stone and brick structures.

▼ *Judgment of Solomon, by Luca Giordano* (Sala del Concistoro).

▲ *Palazzo Chigi-Saracini.*

PALAZZO CHIGI-SARACINI

urther on, on the left, at number 89, stands Palazzo Chigi Saracini, a stone building decorated in brick. In the 13ᵗʰ century, the original nucleus of the house belonged to the Marescotti family, who throughout the 14ᵗʰ century gradually incorporated the neighboring buildings, and, in much the same way as other powerful families of Siena, erected a kind of great, fortified town residence, called the «Castellare». The typically Sienese Gothic architectural elements are

▶ *Inner courtyard of Palazzo Chigi-Saracini.*

▲ *Concert Hall.*

▲ *Adoration of the Magi,*
by Stefano di Giovanni known as Sassetta
(Chigi-Saracini Collection,
Property of the Monte dei Paschi di Siena).

mostly 14th century, but there are several Renaissance additions as well. In 1781, Galgano Saracini enlarged the façade, conforming the whole to the older part. The building was last restored by the painter, architect and sculptor Arturo Vigliardi in 1923 who dedicated much attention to the concert hall. He created a definitely 18th century atmosphere, and even painted a great fresco on the ceiling vault, in the style of Tiepolo, depicting *the Triumphant Return of the Sienese Army after the Battle of Montaperti.* The two modern bronzes that represent Harmony and Melody are by the Sienese sculptor Fulvio Corsini. The transformation was commissioned by Count Guido Saracini, last of his line, so that the famous **Accademia Musicale Chigiana** (Chi-

▲ *Ariadne Abandoned, attributed to Girolamo del Pacchia or Bartolomeo di David*
(Chigi-Saracini Collection, Property of the Monte dei Paschi di Siena).

giana Musical Academy) could have a larger concert hall. The Academy was founded by Count Guido (who died in 1965) and has now become an officially recognized corporate body chaired by the President of the Monte dei Paschi di Siena bank, which partially funds it. The Academy is considered one of the most prestigious in the world, not only because of the high quality of the concerts it presents (the Settimana

◄ *David and Bathsheba, by Bernardino Mei*
(Chigi-Saracini Collection,
Property of the Monte dei Paschi di Siena).

Musicale Chigiana is a well-known festival), but also because of the hundreds of young musicians who flock to Siena every year from all over the world in order to attend the master classes held in Palazzo Chigi Saracini by the most renowned musicians of our time. Thanks chiefly to the generosity of Galgano Saracini, Palazzo Chigi Saracini also contains a large and exceptionally interesting collection of Sienese paintings ranging

◄ *Ceramic plate with Joshua Stopping the Sun, by Ferdinando Maria Campani, c. 1745/50, Manifattura S. Quirico d'Orcia* (Chigi-Saracini Collection, Property of the Monte dei Paschi di Siena).

from the 13th to the 18th century (Sassetta, Sano di Pietro, Beccafumi, Sodoma, etc.). The many rooms of the mansion are furnished and decorated with hundreds of *paintings, sculptures, furniture, objects d'art, porcelain, archaeological finds (Etruscan urns, bucchero, vases* etc.), valuable *musical instruments*, and more.

▼ *The Scarlatti or Beccafumi Room.*

Just beyond Palazzo Chigi Saracini, on the right, we see the imposing **Palazzo Piccolomini**, called *Palazzo delle Papesse*, one of the most perfect examples of Florentine Renaissance architecture, probably built to plans by Rossellino (1460-95) and currently the head quarters of a major Center for Modern and Contemporary Art.

Via di Città ends in **Piazza Postierla** also dubbed "Quattro Cantoni" (the Four Corners), where a marble column, topped by a modern marble statue of the *she-wolf* by Giuliano Vangi marks the Terziere di Città. The modern *little bronze fountain* with an eagle at the top (sculptor Bruno Buracchini), in the square, is one of the seventeen fountains at which the contrade's babies are given their «Contrada Baptism». The little fountain of the Quattro Cantoni is, in fact, where the children of the Noble Contrada of the

▼ *The fountain of the Contrada dell'Aquila in Piazza Postierla.*

▲ *Palazzo Piccolomini ("delle Papesse") in Via di Città.*

▲ *Residence of the Medici Governor.*

Eagle are "baptized" and become full-fledged citizens of the contrada. One of the four corners of the square, the one on the left, towards Via del Capitano, is formed by the two façades of **Palazzo Chigi** then **Piccolomini** (or *Palazzo Chigi-Piccolomini alla Postierla*), which is where the *Superintendent for the Artistic and Historical Assets of* *Siena and Grosseto* has his offices. The splendid mansion was commissioned by Scipione Chigi, towards the second half of the 16th century probably to designs by the painter, sculptor and architect Bartolommeo Neroni, known as "il Riccio". There are two more imposing buildings on Via del Capitano: on the right we have the **Residence of the Medici Governor**, which is used as the Prefecture and as headquarters of the *Provincial Administration*; on the left, the stony façade of **Palazzo del Capitano**, first built at the end of the 13th century as the headquarters of the War Captain and of the Captain of Justice. Like many other Medieval Sienese mansions, this one also underwent major restorations. In 1854, the architect Giulio Rossi headed the restoration project, with totally gratuitous modifications and embellishments to the façade. The ground floor is divided by nine Sienese ogival arches. The upper floor has nine double-mullioned windows. The armorial devices and battlements have all been remade or even invented.

◀ *Palazzo del Capitano.*

▲ *Palazzo Chigi-Piccolomini alla Postierla.*

PIAZZA DEL DUOMO

Via del Capitano leads into Piazza del Duomo, dominated by the marble bulk of one of the most splendid and famous examples of Italian Romanesque-Gothic cathedral architecture. The church we see today (or rather the slightly smaller version formerly constructed on this site) replaced the 9th century **Cathedral of Santa Maria**, built according to a reliable tradition, on the site of a temple dedicated to Minerva.

The façade of the new building that is also dedicated to Our Lady of the Assumption, and is much larger than the 9th century structure, faced towards the Ospedale di Santa Maria della Scala (as it is today). Tradition, supported by fairly credible documentation, affirms that the holy edifice was consecrated with due solemnity on 18 November 1179. This building, too, however, except for the crypt, was totally restructured and enlarged from around 1215-20. The work was done little by little, in order not to interrupt regular services and worship. Moreover, from 1316 onwards, the transept and apse were extended even further. The **bell tower** had al-

ready been grafted onto an existing, short, tower-house belonging to the Bisdomini-Forteguerri family. The **dome** was finished in 1263, when it was covered with lead sheeting and Rosso Padellaio's "apple" or gilded copper sphere was placed on top (the lantern was added much later in 1667 - in the "style" of the cathedral). Today's art critics, basing their opinions on the similarities between the sculptures and decorations of the capitals in the front of the cathedral, the triple window and corbels inside the drum and the work of Nicola Pisano, maintain that the cathedral itself was designed by the Apulian-Pisan artist. The lower part of the façade was both designed and decorated with statuary by Nicola's son, the great Giovanni Pisano, who started working on the project in 1285. The extension of the transept and the elongation of the cathedral towards the choir started, it seems, towards 1316 and continued slowly until about 1339. The work encountered so many technical and stylistic obstacles that in 1332 a commission headed by Lorenzo Maitani, master builder of the Cathedral of Orvieto, decreed that it would be better to rebuild a new church "pulchra magnia et magnifica". The seed for the most ambitious and foolhardy enterprise ever undertaken by the Sienese had been sown, but many years were to elapse before it germinated. It was not until 23 August 1339, in fact, that the General Council of the Bell (Consiglio Generale della Campana) decreed the construction of a vast new temple, in which the existing cathedral was to be included as its transept. The first stone had already been laid some months before

◀ *The bell tower and the dome.*

▲ *The cathedral.*

Piazza
Jacopo
della Quercia

◄ *The sketch shows the new aisles, the bell tower built on the remains of the castle tower, the Romanesque façade and the new apse with its rose window* (from the study by A. Brogi).

and work had started on the three gigantic aisles of the front section which continued up to the Manetti or Santa Maria terrace (piano) and were enclosed by the façade or "Facciatone". The ambitious plans of the Sienese were however disrupted first of all by the terrible Back Death of 1348, which decimated the population, and finally by the collapse of certain essential parts of the construction due to irremediable technical deficiencies, so much so, that in June 1357 the governors of the Republic were not only forced to decree the discontinuation of all work on the New Cathedral, but even had to order the destruction of all parts in danger of collapsing. Important remains of the imposing temple are still visible today in the

◄ *The unfinished façade.*

roofless area to the left of the existing cathedral (known as **Piazza Jacopo della Quercia**), with the columns of the three aisles, its unfinished façade and a part of the left side, where a magnificent doorway (the most beautiful Sienese Gothic doorway and one of the finest in Italy) opens onto the steep staircase leading down to the Baptistry of San Giovanni. After interrupting the construction of the new cathedral, the Sienese turned their attention once more to the old church, which reverted, this time definitely, to its role of Cathedral of Siena. Its façade was only completed towards the end of the 14th century. Work on it recommenced in 1377, under the Master builder Giovanni di Cecco, who attempted to superimpose a late-Gothic top section with the central rose window and three cusps upon the lower late-Romanesque section, spoiling the harmonious development of Giovanni Pisano's architectural elements with the inert spread of the upper section which certainly owes much of its appearance to the Orvieto cathedral façade. Giovanni Pisano, together with helpers and followers, produced a whole series of marble statues of *Saints, Prophets, Sybils* and *Allegorical Beasts* which weave admirably and harmoniously in and out of the design of the lower façade. The figures we see today are nearly all copies of the originals, which have been taken down and placed in the ground floor room in the Museo dell'Opera del Duomo. Giovanni Pisano's great spiraled columns, that used to support the main doorway, have been recently removed to the Crypt of the Statues below and will be replaced by copies. The architrave, sculpted by Tino di Camaino, a follower of Giovanni (c. 1297-1300), represents scenes from the *Life of the Infant Mary with St. Joachim and St. Anne*. The bronze doors with the Glorification of the Virgin are an unpretentious recent work by Enrico Manfrini (1958). Three mediocre mosaic panels by Augusto Castellani to designs by Luigi Mussini and Alessandro Franchi (1877) were set into the cusps at the top of the façade during the 19th century. The mosaics, representing the *Coronation of the Virgin*, the *Birth* and the *Presentation of the Virgin at the Temple*, replaced three gilded bronze reliefs that had been made for the three cusps in 1635. At either end of the parvis stands a column, bearing a she-wolf feeding the Twins, one attributed to the workshop of Giovanni Pisano, the other to Urbano da Cortona (the

▼ *Drawing of the floor of the cathedral, by Giovanni Paciarelli* **(Museo dell'Opera del Duomo).**

▲ *Massacre of the Innocents, marble intarsia by Matteo di Giovanni* (floor of the cathedral).

scenes are partly covered with wooden planks to protect them from the daily wear and tear inflicted by the feet of thousands of visitors and worshippers. Among the scenes always left uncovered is the one showing the *Massacre of the Innocents*, designed by Matteo di Giovanni (1482) and restored in 1790. It is probably the most admired scene on the whole floor, because of its vivid colors and spectacular representation of violent movement.

We can best admire the impressive and lavish interior from the end of the middle aisle. Beneath the gallery there is an endless and somewhat boring line of *popes' heads*, attributed (together with the equally lengthy series of *emperors'* busts) to the workshop of Giovanni di Stefano: they are terra-cotta busts molded in the workshop and fired in the kilns of the Mazzaburroni family starting in 1495 and decorated at the beginning of the 16th century.

The asymmetrical *dome* is supported by six great piers. The two wooden beams resting on the two *central piers* are supposed to have come from the "Carroccio" (War Standard Chariot) used during the

originals, replaced by copies, are also in the Museo dell'Opera). The evocative, severely majestic *interior of the cathedral* is enhanced by the forest of black and white marble striped pillars - the colors of Siena's "Balzana" or arms - which is a motif repeated both inside and outside the building. The black and white marble creates an impression of structural solidity, as well as providing a pictorial chiaroscuro effect, that attenuates the vertical surge of the pillars surmounted by their rounded Romancsquc-likc archcs. Bcforc looking at the various works of art in the church, we should, at this point, pause to admire the unique artistic achievement we are actually standing on, and that covers the whole floor of the cathedral, like some fabulous **carpet**: the 52 panels of inlaid, etched and colored marble. The scenes in the central nave, starting from the entrance, depict *Hermes Trismegistus* (designed by Giovanni di Stefano), *the Sienese She-wolf with the Symbols of the cities allied with Siena* (XIV century), the *Wheel* with the *Imperial Eagle* (XIV century), the *Hill of Virtue* (designed by

Pintoricchio); the *Wheel of Fortune and Power* (designed by Domenico di Niccolò?). The side aisles contain the figures of the Sybils. Except for the well-conserved Hill of Virtues, very little is left of the original panels. The scenes beneath the dome, in the transept and in the apse are much better preserved. The greatest Sienese artists of the 15th and 16th centuries all contributed designs to this remarkable enterprise. Great scenes teeming with hundreds of figures against the bristling towers of fortificd towns and idyllic landscapes unfold beneath our feet. The

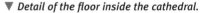

▼ *Detail of the floor inside the cathedral.*

▲ *The spacious nave of the cathedral.*

Battle of Montaperti (1260). Six gigantic gilded plaster statues of *St. Catherine, St. Bernardino* and the other four *Patron Saints* of Siena stand at the top of the six piers. The right transept starts with the Chapel of the Vow, commissioned by Pope Alexander VII (Chigi) and probably designed by Gian Lorenzo Bernini, who was also one of the supervisors of the construction of the Chapel (1659-63). The plan is circular; the Madonna and Child, venerated by

▼ *Statue of Mary Magdalene, by Gian Lorenzo Bernini (Chapel of the Vow).*

▲ *Chapel of the Vow, by Benedetto Giovannelli probably designed by G. Lorenzo Bernini.*

the Sienese as the *Madonna of the Vow* (del Voto), above the altar, is the central portion of a much larger (no longer extant) painting attributed to the workshop of Guido da Siena (c. 1270). The lavishness of the chapel is decidedly Roman Baroque. The *shrine* surrounding the venerated 13th century image, the *gilded bronze angels* and all the *decorations* were designed by Ercole Ferrata of Rome and cast by Giovanni Artusi, called

Piscina. The two large marble statues in the niches at the entrance are masterpieces by Bernini himself, carved in Rome between 1662 and 1663. They represent the *Magdalene* and *St. Jerome*.

The *presbytery* of the cathedral is on a slightly higher level than the aisles and is dominated by the centrally placed imposing marble and bronze **high altar**, upon which stands Vecchietta's magnificent bronze ciborium (1472). Two bronze *candle-bearing angels* stand near the top of the steps leading up to the altar. They are the last admirable works cast by Sassetta's son Giovanni di Stefano (1489). Francesco di Giorgio and Giacomo Cozzarelli made the other two *bronze angels* at the bottom of the steps in 1490 endowing them with the same airy weightlessness they gave the two *little bronze cherub-busts* (called "little spirits") that project from the great masks on each side of the altar. Eight other bronze angels cast in 1551 by D. Beccafumi stand at the side pillars.

The stained-glass rose-window above the apse is of great interest, because of its artistic merits and because it is one of the earliest known examples of Italian stained glass. Carli dates it around 1288 and attributes the cartoon to Duccio, as do many other art histo-

◀ *The stained-glass window by Duccio di Buoninsegna in the apse of the cathedral.*

rians, although some scholars see evidence of the hands of Cimabue and a helper. It used to be in the old apse and was transferred to the new one in 1865. It is divided into nine sections depicting the *Burial*, the *Assumption*, the *Coronation of the Virgin, the Four Evangelists, the Four Patron Saints Ansanus, Savinius, Crescentius* and *Bartholomew*. It is almost a miracle that, after so many centuries of wars and destruction, such an extremely fragile masterpiece should have survived to shed its rainbow light on one of the most beautiful cathedrals in the world. The **choir** (except for the 16th century choir stalls in the apse semicircle) replaces a much earlier 13th century choir, that has been lost. Francesco del Tonghio started working on it alone in 1362 and his son Giacomo joined him in his labors in 1378. Due to 16th century restructuring of the apse, a lot of the earlier ornamentation was

◀ *The apse and the high altar.*

▲ *The choir.*

▲ *The pulpit by Nicola and Giovanni Pisano.*

▲ *Detail of the Nativity and other scenes of the life of the Virgin on the pulpit by Nicola and Giovanni Pisano.*

much richer and more complex (about 307 human figures or heads plus about 70 animal figures or heads have been counted) as well as being less classical and more fervently human in the intense expressive qualities of the faces and attitudes of the figures. A vibrant chiaroscuro and a decided plasticity enhance the profound drama of the scenes (specially where Giovanni's chisel dug into the gleaming marble). The seven main panels on the balustrade, divided by the figures of the *Virgin, Christ, St. Paul,* the *Evangelists* and *Trumpet-blowing Angels* are representations of Episodes in the Life of the Redeemer: the *Nativity,* the *Adoration of the Magi, Presentation at the*

unfortunately lost. The last important work on the choir was done in 1813, when the inlaid marquetry panels by Fra Giovanni da Verona were removed from the magnificent early 16th century choir stalls (which are still preserved in the Abbey church of Monte Oliveto Maggiore near Siena) and attached to the 14th century stalls in the Siena cathedral. An interesting and little known piece of Baroque sculpture can be seen in the *vestibule,* next to the sacristy: the *bronze bust of Alexander VII Chigi,* by Piscina. Beyond the **sacristy**, decorated with frescoes attributed to Benedetto di Bindo (1212), we enter the **Chapter Hall**, hung *with portraits of Sienese popes and bishops.*

Back in the left transept of the cathedral, we find the staggeringly beautiful **pulpit** by Nicola and Giovanni Pisano, the most superb masterpiece in the Cathedral of Siena. A veritable milestone in the history of Italian art, it was, to paraphrase Adolfo Venturi, «the Word of the new art made visible». The great marble complex, covered with figures illustrating the history of the Redemption of Mankind, was started in

Pisa by Nicola on 29 September 1265 and continued in Siena the following year. It was completed by 6 November 1268. Nicola Pisano was helped by his son Giovanni, Arnolfo di Cambio, Donato and Lapo. The three greatest sculptors of their time, Nicola, Giovanni and Arnolfo, worked side by side on this incomparable masterpiece, which although inspired by Nicola's own hexagonal pulpit in the Pisa Baptistery, is so

▼ *Detail with the Adoration of the Magi, panel on the pulpit by Nicola and Giovanni Pisano.*

Temple, the Flight into Egypt, Massacre of the Innocents, Crucifixion, the *Elect,* and the *Damned.*

In the left transept, opposite the Chapel of the Vow, we find the **Chapel of St. John the Baptist**, commissioned by the Rector of the Cathedral Works, Alberto Aringhieri, in 1492, as a worthy *receptacle for the relic* of the Baptist's Arm, preserved in a splendid 15th century silver reliquary and donated to Siena by Pope Pius II. The chapel

▼ *St. John the Baptist, by Donatello* (Chapel of St. John the Baptist).

▲ *The Piccolomini Library.*

was probably designed by Giovanni di Stefano and has a circular floor plan. The magnificent marble *doorway* with statues and reliefs was carved by Marrina but the bases of the two *columns,* richly decorated with classical motifs, are by Antonio Federighi and Giovanni di Stefano. The elegant bronze *gate* is by Sallustio Barili. The great statue of St. *John the Baptist* by Donatello dominates the Chapel from its niche opposite the entrance. It resembles the wooden St. John in Santa Maria Gloriosa dei Frari in Venice and the wooden Magdalen of the Florentine Baptistry. The same dramatic feeling emerges from all their haggard faces, emaciated flesh and from the ragged locks of their hair and hairshirts. In the middle of the chapel there is an octagonal *marble holy water stoup* with eight bas-relief panels by Antonio Federighi (1460). The episodes depicted are: *Creation of Adam and Eve, Temptation of Eve, Appearance of the Almighty, the Expulsion from Eden, Hercules and the Lion, Cacus fighting a Centaur. Cherubs, dolphins, dragons* etc., decorate the base.

We now come to another magnificent architectural, sculptural and frescoed complex made for the cathedral, known as the **Piccolomini Library**. It was commissioned in

1492 by the Archbishop of Siena, Francesco Cardinal Piccolomini Todeschini (later Pope Pius III), who wished to create a worthy receptacle for the fabulous book collection put together by his uncle Pius II, who had died in 1464. The arch on the left, and the bronze *door* by Antoniolo di Giacomo led into the Library, which was never actually used for Pius II's books, but which was dazzlingly frescoed by Pintoricchio all over its ceiling (1502-03) and walls (1505-1507) after the death of pope Pius III. With the help of a large group of assistants, Pintoricchio recounted the more salient events in the Life of Pius II. The picturesque and colorfully portrayed events seize both the humble pilgrim and the scholar with delight. Hundreds of figures mostly

▲ *The Ascension of Christ, miniature by Girolamo da Cremona (Piccolomini Library).*

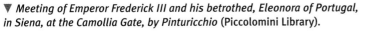

▼ *Meeting of Emperor Frederick III and his betrothed, Eleonora of Portugal, in Siena, at the Camollia Gate, by Pinturicchio (Piccolomini Library).*

in rainbow-hued ceremonial robes (the tints of which are so perfectly preserved, that they seem to have just been painted) throng the walls and are somewhat emotionless but nonetheless spectacular.

The ceiling is decorated in the Roman Renaissance fashion with "grotesques" arranged around the Piccolomini coat of arms. The ten scenes on the walls, starting from the end, right of the window, are: *Enea Silvio Piccolomini, aged 27, leaving for Basle; oration in front of James I of Scotland; Frederick III crowns him Poet Laureate; he bows in submission before the true pope Eugenius IV; as Bishop of Siena he meets Frederick III, betrothed to Eleonora of Portugal at the Camollia Gate of Siena; he is made Cardinal by pope Callixtus III; he is crowned Pope Pius II and his official entrance into the Lateran Basilica; Pius II assembles the Christian princes in Mantua, for the Crusade against the Turks, Pius II canonizes the deceased*

St. Catherine of Siena, on 29 June 1461 (it is said that the youth on the left, in the foreground is a portrait of Raphael and the likeness is in effect quite noticeable); *Arrival of Pius II, already very ill, at the harbor of Ancona to meet the Venetian fleet before its departure for the Crusade.*

He was to die in Ancona, on 15 August 1464 after waiting in vain for the fleet to arrive.

Vasari states that the cartoons for the frescoes were prepared by Raphael. Three drawings in the Uffizi seem to confirm this theory. The marble group of the **Three Graces**

in the center of the Library has been recently restored. It was brought from Rome by Cardinal Todeschini and donated to the Library. It is considered one of the best Roman copies (among the eight known to be in existence) of a Greek painted or sculpted original. The most admired objects in the room, after Pintoricchio's frescoes, are the great missals and antiphonaries in the glass cases beneath the frescoes. The dazzlingly illuminated pages, done partly by great masters of the art such as Liberale di Verona and Girolamo da Cremona, can be considered some of the finest examples of the great Italian illuminators' art of the 15th century.

As we continue our tour of the cathedral we see four statues by Michelangelo Buonarroti on the great marble frontal, known as the **Piccolomini Altar**. Cardinal Piccolomini Todeschini himself commissioned it from the Lombard artist Andrea Bregno (c. 1480), who worked on it with some of his pupils until his death (1501), embellishing it with carved statues and reliefs that recall the works in Santa Maria del Popolo in Rome. It was probably the death of Bregno that induced Cardinal Todeschini to order 15 statues first from Pietro Torrigiani and then from Michelangelo, who, between 1503 and 1504, carved the statues of *St. Peter, St. Paul, St. Pius* and *St. Gregory*. The statues are some of Michelangelo's less known works and we must admit that notwithstanding the plentiful and detailed documentation identifying them as his production, they show Michelangelo at his weakest and most uncertain, which may be due to the fact that he used helpers (specially in the case of St. Pius and St. Gregory). Both St. Peter and St. Paul are more typical of Michelangelo's style, in their vibrant torsion and in the expressive power that seem to herald the dominant force of the Moses of San Pietro in Vincoli in Rome.

▼ *The marble Piccolomini Altar with four statues by Michelangelo* (Cathedral).

OSPEDALE DI S. MARIA DELLA SCALA

The long, low façade of the **Archbishop's Palace** runs along the left side of Piazza del Duomo (if one is facing the cathedral façade). Before 1660 it was the residence of the Rector of the Cathedral Works as well as of the Cathedral Canons, and was connected to the cathedral by a loggia. Opposite the Cathedral is the lengthy façade of the Ospedale di Santa Maria della Scala. This august charitable institution was founded by the cathedral canons in the 9th century, although the first parchment document in which it is officially mentioned dates from 1090. At first, it was merely a hospice, but by the 10th century it was already a hospital run by the Canons and later by lay brothers (Oblates) directed by Comptroller or Rector. The name of Santa Maria della Scala certainly derives from the fact that it abuts on the stairs ("scale" in Italian) leading up to the parvis of Santa Maria, the cathedral. The building is immense, practically a city within the city, where for nearly a thousand years each century has brought additions and changes, although the richly frescoed old 14th-15th century nucleus has been preserved. Two highly interesting rooms have been converted into a museum: the **old sacristy**, entirely decorated with

▲ *The varicolored Archbishop's Palace overlooking Piazza del Duomo.*

▲ *Right façade of the Ospedale di Santa Maria della Scala.*

◀ *The old sacristy with frescoes by Vecchietta.*

▲ *Granting the Statutes,
by Domenico di Bartolo
(the "pilgrims' hall").*

frescoes by Vecchietta, and the large "**pilgrims' hall**". The frescoes in this room, by Vecchietta, Priamo della Quercia and Domenico di Bartolo around 1444, portray the *glory*, the *power* and the *charitable deeds* of the hospital. This fresco cycle, one of the few dealing with a secular-civic theme, is, therefore, of exceptional artistic and historical interest. The present **Church of the Hospital**, dedicated to Our Lady of the Assumption, is an enlarged, or rather totally reconstructed 15th century edition of a much smaller Medieval church. The airy, simple interior fits beautifully into the aisleless Sienese Renaissance structure, reminiscent of the Franciscan Gothic tradition. The high altar, a fascinating architectural and sculptural complex, bears an imposing bronze *Resurrected Christ* (1476) by Vecchietta, that replaces the ciborium by the same artist, transferred to the high altar of the cathedral in 1506. The statue is one of the finest of the Sienese Renaissance. It has a dramatic strength

▶ *Enlarging the Hospital
of S. Maria della Scala,
by Domenico di Bartolo
(the "pilgrims' hall").*

▲ *Receiving Foundlings and Marriage of the Foundlings, by Domenico di Bartolo* (the "pilgrims' hall").

reminiscent of Donatello, combined with exquisite anatomical technique and vigorous luminous qualities. The two bronze *angel candelabra* on the steps below were cast (1585) by Accursio Baldi da Monte San Savino, earning Giambologna's admiration and praise. The spacious *apse semicircle*, once frescoed by Francesco di Giorgio Martini, was enlarged and refrescoed in 1732 by the Neapolitan painter Sebastiano Conca, who painted the *Pool of Bethesda* in a perspective colonnade. A little door leads out of the choir into the sacristy-treasure vault, where a large number of relics are kept in precious gold or silver *reliquaries* made by Byzantine (11th-12th century) and 15th-16th century Sienese goldsmiths.

▼ *Taking Care of the Sick (detail), by Domenico di Bartolo* (the "pilgrims' hall").

► *King David, by Carlo Andrea Galletti* (Church of the Ospedale di S. Maria della Scala).

▼ *Reliquary box, 14th century* (Ospedale di S. Maria della Scala).

▲ *Reliquary of S. Cristina, 15th cent.* (Ospedale di S. Maria della Scala).

▼ *Resurrected Christ, by Vecchietta* (Church of the Ospedale di S. Maria della Scala).

▲ *Madonna and Child (detail), by Paolo di Giovanni Fei* (Ospedale di S. Maria della Scala).

Museo Archeologico Nazionale di Siena

Some of the rooms of the Ospedale di S. Maria della Scala house the **Museo Archeologico Nazionale di Siena** (the entrance is from Piazza del Duomo and the corner of Via del Capitano). The museum contains hundreds of objects of outstanding artistic-historical interest from the prehistoric, Etruscan and Roman periods that were collected throughout the area surrounding Siena.

▲ *Etruscan fibula.*

▼ *Etruscan pottery, 4th cent. BC.*

MUSEO DELL'OPERA DEL DUOMO

The right aisle of the New Cathedral was transformed as early as the 15th century into the headquarters of the Opera (Cathedral Works). Nearly all the rooms inside are now used for the Museo dell'Opera del Duomo, which is chiefly famous for Giovanni Pisano's marble statues and for the great altarpiece with Duccio di Buoninsegna's Maestà.

Most of the ground floor is occupied by architectural fragments and by the great marble statues carved by Giovanni (1284-96) and his followers for the cathedral façade: strong dramatic figures of *Prophets, Sybils, Philosophers*, impetuously launched forward or drawn back, with powerful muscles draped in flowing robes. An awesome concert of violently agitated

▼ *A room in the Museo dell'Opera with sculpture by Giovanni Pisano, Jacopo della Quercia and Donatello.*

◀ *St. Simeon (det.), by Giovanni Pisano.*

figures, that nearly all express tragedy or terror, in gesture or expression: *Moses, Plato, Simeon, Elijah, Balaam, Miriam, Habbakkuk.* Even the animals seem to explode with tension in the complexity of their violent, almost tragic masks that belong to a lost world of giants. The **Duccio Room**, upstairs, can almost be termed a Holy of Holies of Sienese painting. After many vicissitudes, the imposing

▼ *Maestà, by Duccio di Buoninsegna (front) and detail.*

Being led to Pilate	Flagellation	Way to Calvary	Crucifixion	Burial	The Three Maries at the Sepulcher	Christ at Emmaus
Before Herod	Crowning with Thorns	Pilate Washing his Hands		Deposition from the Cross	Christ in Limbo	Noli me tangere
Entry into Jerusalem	Washing of Feet	Pact of Judas	Taking of Christ	Before Annas	Derision of Christ	To the Praetor
	Last Supper	Discourse after the Supper	Garden of Olives	Peter's First Denial	Before Caiaphas	Before Pilate

Duccio **Maestà** has been placed here. It was commissioned from Duccio on the 9 October 1308 and the great panel was painted on both sides as well as with a predella and cusp decorations.

Nearly all the painting was done by Duccio himself, as the contract stipulated. The front panel shows the *Virgin Mary*, Protectress of Siena, *with her Son on her knees, seated on a throne and surrounded by a throng of Angels and Saints.* The first four kneeling figures are the Patron Saints of Siena: *Saints Ansanus, Savinius, Crescentius and Victor.* The predella contains seven little scenes from the *Life of the Virgin and the Infancy of Christ spaced by the figures of Prophets.* The cusps are decorated with further *Episodes from the Life of the Virgin.*

▲ *Maestà, by Duccio di Buoninsegna (back) with scenes of the Life and Passion of Christ.*

▼ *Kiss of Judas, detail of the Maestà (back).*

◀ *The Three Maries at the Sepulcher, detail of the Maestà (back).*

▼ *Madonna and Child, by Duccio di Buoninsegna, from the Pieve of Crevole.*

▲ *Noli me tangere, detail of the Maestà (back).*

▲ *Christ at Emmaus, detail of the Maestà (back).*

The other side, that used to face the choir, contains many *Scenes from the Life of Christ*. Even in its present stripped state, Duccio's Maestà is still one of the turning points of European culture at the beginning of the 14th century, when profound transformations affected every aspect of Western cultural mores. Where Giotto or Dante and even Giovanni Pisano opened up vistas of unhoped-for human, albeit dramatic, earthly understanding, Duccio turned his attention towards a musical harmony between heaven and earth, shaking off the chains that had hitherto bound painting and Byzantine culture in general and directed his art towards more concrete form, both in his transcendent poetic dreams of divine light, which he expresses in the gleaming gold and lucid purity of his colors, as well as in the human reality of his solidly composed figures and their severely solemn expressions. Another masterpiece from the cathedral is preserved in the Duccio Room: the *Birth of the Virgin*, by Pietro Lorenzetti, signed and dated 1342. Pietro almost anticipates the perspective studies of the following century and offers us a scene that is based on skilfully measured space

▼ *Birth of the Virgin, by Pietro Lorenzetti.*

▼ *Madonna and Child,
by Jacopo della Quercia.*

(breaking with the triptych tradition) and each figure is portrayed in a combination of grace and solemnity. St. Anne is shown in the reclining position typical of the statues of the deceased on Etruscan sarcophagi. In the two neighboring rooms leading out of the Duccio room there are various interesting relics and artworks linked to the history of the Cathedral of Siena. Five gilded wooden statues from the Church of San Martino, representing the *Madonna and Child, Saints Bartholomew, Anthony Abbot, John the Baptist and John the Evangelist*, attributed to Jacopo della Quercia and Giovanni da Imola have been placed in the vestibule of the room to the right. Jacopo and his workshop are also supposed to have carved the much discussed polychrome wooden statue of St. John the Baptist, which comes from the Church of San Giovanni. The Treasure Room contains a large collection of gold and silver artifacts, most of which come from the cathedral, even if the most precious and fascinating of all is the **Reliquary of the Head of St. Galgano**, that originally came from the great Cistercian Abbey of San Galgano. This precious octagonal, cusped, shrine-shaped object chiseled in a style that is already Gothic, was made of gilded, embossed and filigree silver in the 13th century, almost certainly by French craftsmen. Pope Alexander VII Chigi gave the Metropolitan Cathedral of Siena a

golden Rose Bush (end case) which is similar to, the one given by Pope Pius II Piccolomini to the Senate of the Sienese Republic in 1458, although it is more elaborate in the branches, leaves and roses.

◀ *St. John the Baptist,
by Jacopo
della Quercia*

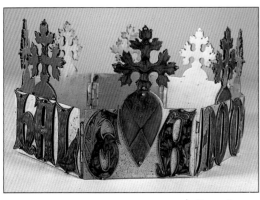

► The golden rose
of Pope Alexander VII Chigi.

▲ Crown known
as of "S. Galgano",
by a Sienese goldsmith
(first half 14th cent.).

◄ The crosier
of S. Galgano,
Sienese gold work
(around 1320).

▼ Wooden crucifix, by Giovanni Pisano.

▼ Fifteenth century chalice
by the goldsmith Goro
di Ser Neroccio.

▲ Reliquary of "St. Galgano" (S. Galgano).

◀ *Madonna and Child
Enthroned with Saints,
by Matteo di Giovanni.*

▲ *Madonna and Child Enthroned, with Angels
and Saints Anthony of Padua and Bernardino
of Siena (1460), by Matteo di Giovanni.*

◀ *Madonna of the Large Eyes,
by the Maestro di Tressa.*

The last two rooms of the museum have been placed almost at the end of the left aisle of the "New Cathedral" so that we have a close-up view of the windows and magnificent capitals on the black and white pillars that were incorporated into the walls. The last room of the Museo dell'Opera contains a number of paintings, some of which can be considered absolute masterpieces. It is called the room of the *Madonna of the large eyes (occhi grossi)* or Madonna of the Victory of Montaperti. The importance to Siena of this venerable relic (the central part of an altarpiece) is certainly significant, if, as appears likely, this was the image on the high altar of the cathedral, in front of which the Sienese vowed they would present the keys of the city to the Virgin (on the eve of the Battle of Montaperti, 4 September 1260) if they should be victorious against the Florentines, which in fact they were. Two other fine paintings in this room are the delightful little panels by Sano di Pietro (c. 1444), *showing St. Bernardino preaching in Piazza San Francesco and in Piazza del Campo*. The latter is particularly fascinating, because the scene in front of Palazzo Pubblico is as minutely detailed as an illuminated manuscript, with its groups of no-

bles and commoners listening devoutly to the saint. The larger group of the women is separated from the men by a long red curtain; the white shawls and veils draped over their heads half conceal splendid long, embroidered red, black or green gowns. Sano even painted the shutters on the windows, which enabled people to see, without being seen, as well as the famous enclosure with its ladder, where a live she-wolf was kept as a symbol of the mythical origins of Siena.

► *St. Bernardino Preaching in Piazza del Campo, by Sano di Pietro.*

THE BAPTISTRY OF SAN GIOVANNI

After the apse of the Cathedral was lengthened, abutting on the cliff over Valle Piatta, great arches were built beneath it, starting in 1316, underneath which, like a crypt, the church of San Giovanni Battista was created. This new structure used as the Baptistry of Siena was probably designed by Camaino di Crescentino. The six vaults of the cathedral above were completed after the work on the new cathedral was suspended, whilst the decoration of the façade of San Giovanni was continued for decades, under the direction of Domenico di Agostino, starting in 1355. The top part of the façade was never finished, but the rest is in pure Sienese Gothic style, with three deeplysplayed jambed doorways, above which runs a gallery of arches and a frieze supporting three great twin ogival mullioned windows (1355). The three graffito scenes on the floor of the parvis portray the *Birth of a Child*, the *Baptism* and the *Blessing* (or Confirmation?) of *Six Children*.

The interior of San Giovanni is rectangular, divided into three aisles by two large pillars. All the vaults were completely frescoed in the 15th century; the most remarkable frescoes are the ones covering the central vault, by Vecchietta (1450), depicting the *Apostles* and the *Articles of the Creed*. The great master-

▲ *Drawing for the façade of the baptistry of San Giovanni. (Museo dell'Opera del Duomo).*

◀ *The façade of the baptistry of San Giovanni.*

piece, that makes Siena the envy of the world, however, is the **Baptismal Font** in the center of the church. It has often been called the "oldest anthology of early Italian Renaissance sculpture." In addition to contributions by a number of less famous artists, this masterpiece is the work of the hands of three of the greatest sculptors of the time Donatello, Lorenzo Ghiberti and Jacopo della Quercia. The base consists of two great hexagonal marble

▲ *Baptismal font in the baptistry of San Giovanni.*

▲ *Annunciation to Zacharias,*
by Jacopo della Quercia
(detail of the baptismal font).

Herod (Donatello); and *Fortitud*e (Goro di Neroccio). The most impressive of all the scenes is the Donatello relief: a vortex with the head of the Baptist in the center, draws the figures together yet freezes their movements. It creates a dramatic feeling that is echoed, after the perspective hiatus of the laden tables, by the tragic amazement of the observers on the right. In the background, in an incredible perspective fugue created with a depth of but a few millimeters, the life of the court continues unperturbed, acted out by timeless figures, under the receding arches.

▼ *The Baptist before Herod,*
by Lorenzo Ghiberti
(detail of the baptismal font).

steps; the marble font itself is hexagonal too. The six sides, separated from each other by six gilded bronze figures of the *Virtues*, contain six gilded bronze panels depicting Episodes from the Life of St. John the Baptist in chronological order: *Zacharias being told of the forthcoming birth of the Baptist* (Jacopo della Quercia); statuette of *Justice* (Giovanni di Turino); *Birth of the Baptist* (Turino di Sano and Giovanni di Turino); statuette of *Charity* (Giovanni di Turino); the *Baptist Preaching* (Giovanni di Turino), statuette of *Prudence* (Giovanni di Turino), the *Baptism of Christ* (Lorenzo Ghiberti); *Faith* (Donatello); the *Baptist before Herod* (Lorenzo Ghiberti); *Hope* (Donatello); the *Head of the Baptist presented to*

As we walk back along Via del Capitano, we come to Piazza Postierla and the beginning of Via di San Pietro. The two mansions which used to belong to the Brigidi and Buonsignori families have now become the Pinacoteca Nazionale (National Picture Gallery), one of the greatest Italian Museums, especially for the "fondi oro" or paintings on golden backgrounds of the

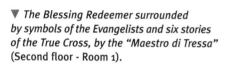

▼ *The Blessing Redeemer surrounded by symbols of the Evangelists and six stories of the True Cross, by the "Maestro di Tressa" (Second floor - Room 1).*

The altar dossal is dated 1215.

▲ *Home of the Pinacoteca Nazionale, in Via di San Pietro.*

Sienese 14th and 15th centuries. The Sienese painting tradition from Duccio di Buoninsegna to the Lorenzetti, from Simone Martini to Sassetta, Francesco di Giorgio or Giovanni di Paolo (including Neroccio, Matteo di Giovanni, Sodoma and Beccafumi) is presented in chronological order, offering a fabulous series of masterpieces and minor works and a unique insight into the evolution of painting in Siena. The events that led up to the formation of this important collection came to a head on 15 May, 1930 when a decree was issued officially authorizing the transfer of the Na-

◀ *St. Peter Enthroned and stories of his life and of the life of Christ, attributed to Guido di Graziano (Second floor - Room 2).*

This may be the most important work in Siena around the seventh-eighth decade of the 13th century.

▲ *Entry in Jerusalem (detail) by Guido da Siena, 13th century* (Second floor - Room 1).

tional Picture Gallery of Siena to its present site in Via San Pietro. The Buonsignori palace, however, already appears too small for the size and importance of the collection. The authorities are considering transferring the works to the Ospedale di Santa Maria della Scala, in Piazza del Duomo, which is already a museum in itself. A tour of the Pinacoteca Nazionale of Siena starts on the second floor. Further information on the works in the gallery can be obtained from: P. Torriti, *La Pinacoteca Nazionale di Siena, I dipinti dal XII al XV secolo*, Sagep, Genoa 1977, P. Torriti, *La Pinacoteca Nazionale di Siena*, edizione Sagep, Genoa 1990.

▼ *Madonna and Child with Saints, by Duccio di Buoninsegna and workshop* (Second floor - Room 3).

The high quality of the central panel betrays the hand of Duccio, while the side panels seem to be the work of a collaborator.

▼ *Adoration of the Magi, by Bartolo di Fredi*
(Second floor - Room 5).

▲ *The Madonna of the Franciscans, by Duccio di Buoninsegna*
(Second floor - Room 4).

Tiny as it its, the open spatial composition of this picture combines a solemn monumentality with a particularly elegant line. This masterpiece of thirteenth and fourteenth century painting reveals the hand of a young Duccio with clear references to Cimabue.

◄ *Blessed Agostino Novelli and four of his miracles (1339), by Simone Martini*
(Second floor - Room 6).

The charming stories with the miracles of the saint show: the healing of a child attacked by a wolf, the saving of a child who fell from a balcony, the saving of a horseman who fell in a ravine, the healing of a child who fell from the cradle.

▼ *Madonna and Child, by Simone Martini*
(Second floor - Room 6).

Originally in the parish church
of Lucignano d'Arbia, this picture by Simone,
one of his purest and most charming
depictions of women, was formerly
hidden under crude late 16th century
overpainting. The obvious similarities
with the polyptych in the museum
in Orvieto and the one in the museum
in Pisa date the picture to around 1321.

▶ *Madonna and Child,
attributed to Simone Martini*
(Second floor - Room 6).

Traditionally attributed to Duccio,
the picture has recently been assigned
to the young Simone Martini, on account
of the fluid and delicate line,
which recalls the famous "Maestà"
in the Palazzo Pubblico.

▲ *Madonna of Mercy, by Simone Martini
and Memmo di Filippuccio*
(Second floor - Room 6).

This work is particularly important
in the study of Sienese art between
Duccio di Buoninsegna and Simone Martini.

◀ Annunciation, by Ambrogio Lorenzetti
(Second floor - Room 7).

Signed and dated 1344, this is the last
known work by Ambrogio, who painted
it for the Magistrates of the Biccherna
of the Commune of Siena.

▼ *Madonna and Child, by Ambrogio Lorenzetti (det.)*
(Second floor - Room 7).

This picture, known as the "Small Maestà",
is one of Ambrogio's finest works, almost comparable
to a miniature.

▲ *Madonna and Child, by Ambrogio Lorenzetti* (Second floor - Room 7).

This is one of Ambrogio's most typical female figures, close to the so-called
"Madonna del latte" (Nursing Madonna or "Madonna of the Milk")
in the Museo Diocesano in Siena.

▲ *Madonna and Child Enthroned,*
Angels and Saints (det.),
by Pietro Lorenzetti
(Second floor - Room 7).

▼ *Sobach's Dream*
(detail of the predella
of the Madonna and Child
Enthroned, Angels and Saints),
by Pietro Lorenzetti
(Second floor - Room 7).

This is the Carmine altarpiece.
It was commissioned by the Carmelites
of Siena, and was finished by Pietro
in 1329 as attested by the documents
and the signature with the date.
Unfortunately it is incomplete
for the two side wings and at least
one cusp are in American museums.
Even so the altarpiece itself represents
one of the outstanding moments
in painting in the Italian fourteenth
century, both thanks to its regal
monumentality of the larger panels,
and in the fineness of the details
and the description of the marvelous
landscapes in the predella.

► *Madonna of Humility, by Domenico di Bartolo* (Second floor - Room 9).

Signed and dated 1433, with lovely Latin hexameters. In this panel, to be considered one of the finest expressions of the Sienese Renaissance, Domenico di Bartolo was aware of the vibrant art of the early Donatello and the solid reality of the putti in Luca della Robbia's famous choir loft, but even more probably the very human children by Masaccio, in a sense heralding the developments of Filippo Lippi and Domenico Veneziano.

◄ *Birth of the Virgin and Saints, by Paolo di Giovanni Fei (late 14th century)* (Second floor - Room 7).

◀ *Mystic Marriage of St. Catherine
of Alexandria, by Michelino da Besozzo*
(Second floor - Room 9).

One of the most significant works
of the International Gothic in Italy.

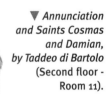

▼ *Annunciation
and Saints Cosmas
and Damian,
by Taddeo di Bartolo*
(Second floor -
Room 11).

◀ *St. Michael Enthroned and Saints Anthony Abbot and John
the Baptist (det.), by Angelo Puccinelli da Lucca* (Second floor - Room 9).

A rare and precious work with brilliant flashes of gold by this artist
from Lucca who was active in Siena around 1360-65.

▲ *Polyptych of San Galgano (detail of the predella), by Giovanni di Paolo* (Second floor - Room 12).

▼ *Flight into Egypt, by Giovanni di Paolo* (Second floor - Room 13).

Except for the two small columns and the central crucifixion, the other side panels and the predella were part of a dismembered polyptych known as of San Galgano. The most fascinating scenes are in the predella, in the highly poetical representation of the landscape with cold ashen tones, in imitation of the barren Sienese "crete", and in the figures where the artist "succeeds in compensating for the transitory defects of execution, and presents us with desolate, decrepit images which seem to rise from the abyss of the void, as large as oriental genii and mute as shades, like the lengthening shadows of evening" (Brandi, 1949).

▲ *Last Judgment (det.), by Giovanni di Paolo* (Second floor - Room 13).

The large predella reveals
the characteristics of a mature Giovanni,
with a lively fantasy and an exceptionally
pure and fine line.

▼ *Presentation in the Temple,
by Giovanni di Paolo*
(Second floor - Room 13).

The imposing splendid altarpiece
was commissioned by the
chancellors of the Corporazione
dei Pizzicaioli in 1447 from
Giovanni di Paolo for their
chapel in the church of S. Maria
della Scala in Siena.

◀ *Madonna of Humility, by Giovanni di Paolo* (Second floor - Room 13).

This is one of Giovanni di Paolo's best known and most admired compositions, in particular for the indefinite landscape composed on a circular horizon seen from above (as always in Sienese fourteenth century painting) the better to define the details which are thus all visualized in a brilliant light which lends life to, but then immediately crystallizes, the tenuous colors. Despite intimations of perspective the space remains as unreal and poetical as the bright halo around the humble figure of the Virgin.

▼ *Madonna and Child with Saints Jerome and Bernardino, by Neroccio di Bartolommeo* (Second floor - Room 14).

The artist has personalized precedent influences, presenting us with what may be his masterpiece. It is unquestionably one of the finest pictures of the Sienese fifteenth century. If the most recent inspiration comes from a painting by Matteo di Giovanni, the roots of this suave Madonna certainly go back to the lyrical silhouettes of Simone Martini, all of a hundred and fifty years earlier.

◀ *Madonna and Child with Angels, by Francesco di Giorgio Martini* (Second floor - Room 14).

The angel with its blonde mass of hair may be the loveliest this Sienese artist ever created. The Madonna, thoughtfully gazing off into the distance, has also been drawn with a linear elegance and a plasticity that is delicate in its chiaroscuro, but as full and vigorous as Verrocchio and Botticelli.

*◀ Madonna and Child with four saints,
by Neroccio di Bartolommeo (Second floor - Room 14).*

*▲ Annunciation, by Francesco di Giorgio Martini
(Second floor - Room 14).*

The artist now deliberately renounces a more rational
perspective solution for a more lyrical vision of reality.

*◀ Nativity with Saints Bernard and Thomas,
by Francesco di Giorgio Martini (Second floor - Room 14).*

This is the only work the artist signed. No longer
dependant on his collaboration with Neroccio,
the artist now expresses himself in a clearly
Florentine idiom, under the influence of Verrocchio.
In the general layout and in the details, in the decisive
line, the classical landscape, the altarpiece displays
an unyielding firmness with reflections of northern art,
of Mantegna, via Liberale da Verona
and Girolamo da Cremona.

▲ *Above, Saint Anthony Beaten by the Devils and, below, the Last Supper, by Stefano di Giovanni known as "Sassetta"*
(Second floor - Room 15bis).

Fragments of the lost Altarpiece of the Arte della Lana, painted by the young Sassetta between 1423 and 1424 and a fundamental piece for the study of the Sienese fifteenth century. (The other fragment with the monk Hus burned at the stake is in the National Gallery in Melbourne).

A city on the sea, attributed to Stefano di Giovanni known as "Sassetta" (Second floor - Room 15bis).

A fascinating vision, in the purity of design and the skilful touch of the highlights, once attributed to Ambrogio Lorenzetti but now more rightfully considered a fifteenth century work and thought to be by Sassetta. It was probably part of a larger complex, such as, for example, the door of a wardrobe or of the Altarpiece of the Arte della Lana.

▲ *St. Jerome in the Desert, by Sano di Pietro* (Second floor - Room 16).

One of Sano's paintings closest in style to the Maestro dell'Osservanza.

▲ *The Sick Man in the Big Bed (detail of the predella with scenes from the life of Saints Cosmas and Damian, by Sano di Pietro* (Second floor - Room 17).

▲ *Apparition of the Madonna to Pope Calixtus III, by Sano di Pietro* (Second floor - Room 17).

◀ *Madonna and Child Enthroned, Angels and Saints, by Sano di Pietro* (Second floor - Room 16).

Polyptych of the Jesuits, signed and dated 1444. This is Sano's first sure work and his masterpiece. The predella is in the Louvre. We know nothing of Sano's activity prior to 1444 (remember that Sano was born in 1406), unless, prior to 1444 the so-called "Maestro dell'Osservanza" and Sano are one and the same person.

▼ *Elisabeth of England,*
by Quentin Massys the Younger
(First floor - Room 24).

▲ *Coronation of the Virgin, by Francesco di Giorgio Martini and collaborator*
(Second floor - Room 19).

Imposing altarpiece in which the artist comes close to contemporary
Florentine painting, in particular Verrocchio, but also to his fellow artist
Neroccio di Bartolommeo, in his sinuous line. The artist, in the full fifteenth century,
provides us with a spectacular treatment of the surface forms, with a superimposition
of elongated uneasy shapes, almost harking back to the pure lyricism
of Simone Martini.

▼ *Blessed Sienese of the so-called "Arliquiera"*
(detail of the figure of St. Catherine),
by Lorenzo di Pietro known as "Vecchietta"
(Second floor - Room 19).

▲ *Ransom of the Prisoners,*
by Girolamo Genga (First floor - Room 23).

Detached fresco, from the Palazzo
del Magnifico Pandolfo Petrucci in Siena,
decorated around 1509.

▼ *The Visitation of Mary and St. Elisabeth*
with Saints Anthony Abbot, Anthony of Padua,
John the Baptist, Nicholas of Bari, Thomas Aquinas
and Leonard, by Pietro degli Orioli
(First floor - Room 23).

▲ *Holy Family with the Young St. John,*
by Bernardino di Betto known as Pintoricchio
(First floor - Room 23).

One of Pintoricchio's most famous paintings
as well as one of the most popular works
in the Gallery.

▲ *The Stigmata of St. Catherine of Siena, by Domenico Beccafumi*
(First floor - Room 27).

From the destroyed convent of Monteoliveto at Porta Tufi in Siena. The first youthful masterpiece of the greatest 16th century Sienese painter.

▼ *Birth of the Virgin (det.), by Beccafumi*
(First floor - Room 29).

Masterpiece of the late period of "Mecherino", mentioned by Vasari in his "Lives", together with the predella now in the Asquith Collection in Mells (Somerset, England).

◀ *Christ at the Column, by Giovanni Antonio Bazzi known as Sodoma* (First floor - Room 31).

Fragment of a large fresco in the cloister of the Convent of S. Francesco in Siena.

◀ *Nativity of Christ with an Angel and the young St. John, by Giovanni Antonio Bazzi known as Sodoma* (First floor - Room 32).

From the convent of Lecceto, near Siena.

▲ *Ghismunda, by Bernardino Mei*
(First floor - Room 33).

◀ *Deposition from the Cross,*
by Giovanni Antonio Bazzi known
as Sodoma (First floor - Room 32).

Magnificent masterpiece by this noble
artist, who came to Siena from Vercelli
in the late fifteenth century and was
active in Tuscany in the early decades
of the sixteenth century. The work
is from the Cinuzzi chapel in the church
of S. Francesco in Siena.

▶ *St. Jerome, by Albrecht Dürer*
(Third floor - Spannocchi Collection).

The poor state of conservation
of the work up to not long ago led
to various theories regarding attribution
and authenticity. Recent restoration
revealed the high quality of the painting
which now can be fairly certainly
assigned to the great master of Nuremberg.

◀ *St. Michael Driving Down the Rebel
Angels, by Domenico Beccafumi*
(First floor - Room 37).

This is one of Beccafumi's masterpieces,
even though unfinished. It was painted
for the church of the Carmine but was
rejected, apparently due to the nudity
of the rebel angels, and replaced by
a more chaste version. Art historians
generally agree on a date around 1528.

◄ *Nativity of Christ, by Lorenzo Lotto*
(Third floor - Spannochi collection).

The light emanates from the Child
and illuminates the figures, flickering
faintly in the background in a magic
yet highly naturalistic vision.

▼ *Annunciation, by Paris Bordone*
(Third floor - Spannochi collection).

▲ *The Tower of Babel, by an unknown Flemish painter of the first half of the 16th century* (Third floor - Spannochi collection).

◀ *The Game of Morra, by Jean du Champ (?), also variously attributed to others, ranging from Cecco del Caravaggio to Antiveduto Gramatica* (Currently to be seen in the storerooms of the Gallery).

THE CHURCH OF S. NICCOLÒ AL CARMINE

Via San Pietro leads into Piazza di Postierla («I quattro Cantoni» or the «Four Corners»). On the corner, opposite Palazzo Borghesi, which used to contain frescoes by Beccafumi (now lost), is a *pharmacy* containing interesting neoclassical furniture, designed by Agostino Fantastici, around 1830. Turning immediately left, we enter *Via di Stalloreggi* ("Stabulae Regis" or "Stables of the king"?), almost completely lined with *medieval mansions* built of brick or stone (where the towers of the Cacciaconti used to stand), which are often very interesting, as they have not undergone much restructuring and still preserve most of their original appearance. Midway down the street (at the corner of Via Castelvecchio) there is a shrine with the *Virgin holding the Dead Jesus* (this work by Sodoma is also known as the Virgin of the Crow). At the end of Via Stalloreggi, there is a gateway or arch, in the right pier of which a 16th century *shrine*, surrounded by a delicate stucco frame, encloses a frescoed *Madonna and Child, with Sts. John the Baptist and Catherine of Siena*, attributed to

▲ *Shrine of the Virgin of the Crow, with a fresco by Sodoma.*

◀ *The Church of S. Niccolò al Carmine.*

▲ *The Arch of the Two Gates, at the end of Via di Stalloreggi.*

Nicola Nasini (1710) depicting scenes illustrating the *Carmelite Rule*. The **bell tower**, recently attributed to Peruzzi, actually seems to date from 16th century, although some scholars consider it a 17th century structure. The Carmelite Church has remained reasonably intact in spite of the 19th century expropriations, and the radical restructuring

▼ *Expulsion of the Rebel Angels,*
by Domenico Beccafumi
(Church of S. Niccolò
al Carmine).

Bartolomeo di David (16th century). Left of the arch, a plaque indicates that Duccio di Buoninsegna used to live in the house (probably after and not before painting the famous «Maestà», which "was painted in the Muciatti house outside the Stalloreggi gate", according to contemporary sources. The gateway was part of the oldest circle of the town walls and consisted of two great arches (one of which was walled up centuries ago), but the gate is still known as the *Arch of the Two Gates* (Arco delle due Porte). The oldest shrine in the city is set into the outer face of the town wall; it encloses a 14th century frescoed *Madonna and Child*. Leaving the archway, we turn left into the *Pian dei Mantellini* surrounded by churches and fine mansions. Of special note: the great complex of the *Carmelite Monastery* with the adjacent Church of **San Niccolò al Carmine**. The first documented proof of the **Carmelite Order's** presence in Siena and of the foundation of a church of theirs is dated 1262. The existing church was constructed through the 14th, 15th and 16th centuries and subjected to restoration and additions up to the present. The restored **Cloister** (No. 44), built at the end of the 16th century, contains frescoes by Giuseppe

at the beginning of the 20th century and contains many works of art. See especially: the large panel by Domenico Beccafumi, showing *St. Michael pursuing the rebellious angels*, painted before 1535 and a second, expurgated version of the unfinished panel, now in the Pinacoteca Nazionale, both of which are, at any rate, fundamentally important works of the Tuscan Mannerist school. The predella underneath is not original, but a mediocre contribution by Stefano Volpi. The sacristy contains a beautiful polychrome terra-cotta statue of *St. Sigismund*, attributed rightly to Giacomo Cozzarelli in his later years (c. 1506).

The Carmelite Church stands near the turning from Pian dei Mantellini into *Via della Diana*, which takes its name from the spring that was sought for in vain by the Sienese, as Dante Alighieri recalls. The *Via di S. Marco* is almost parallel to it; at the beginning of the street on the left, is the little Romanesque façade in black and white stone, of the deconsecrated *church of San Marco*, which is now used as a shop.

The intersection of Via di San Marco and Via della Diana is marked by the delightful little 18th century façade of the **Chapel of Our Lady of the Rosary**. The façade of the chapel is intact and is an interesting example of Sienese Baroque. Romagnoli has attributed its design to Pietro Augusto Montini (1722-23), while Chierici maintains that it was the work of Jacopo Franchini. The travertine Renaissance *well* in front of the chapel was commissioned by Francesco Cardinal Petrucci in 1522.

◄ *The seventeenth century façade of the Chapel of the Madonna of the Rosary.*

▲ *Via S. Marco at the corner with Via della Diana.*

THE CHURCH OF SANT'AGOSTINO

Via delle Cerchia connects Pian dei Mantellini with the **Prato di Sant'Agostino**, near the *Porta all'Arco* (Gateway of the Arch). It is a typical street that follows the line of the medieval walls. The imposing bulk of the Church of Sant'Agostino, the apse of which is still Romanesque, was started towards the middle of the 13th century (1258). Construction, however, was still in progress in 1309. We do not know exactly when work was concluded, but we do know that the church was enlarged and restructured between 1450 and 1458/90. Several important traces of

▼ *The Church of S. Agostino.*

▲ *Crucifixion, by Pietro Perugino.*

▲ *Adoration of the Kings, by Sodoma.*

(more specifically) Sienese 13th-17th century masters. The outstanding works include, the *Crucifixion*, by Perugino; the *Baptism of Constantine*, by F. Vanni; the *Holy Trinity*, by P. Sorri; the **Bichi Chapel** frescoed by F. di Giorgio Martini and Signorelli; **the Piccolomini Chapel** with A. Lorenzetti's *Madonna Enthroned* and the *Adoration of the Magi*, by Sodoma, etc.

▲ *Fresco in the Piccolomini Chapel, by Ambrogio Lorenzetti.*

▼ *Madonna and Child, attributed to Giovanni di Turino.*

this second period are visible on the outer walls of the Augustinian Monastery adjacent to the church, as well as inside the church itself, in the last chapel on the right in the transept, which was restored to its original state a few years ago. The overall impression conveyed by the interior as we see it today, however, is predominantly neoclassical, because of the work done by Luigi Vanvitelli in 1755, after the disastrous 1747 fire. He renovated the building and endowed it with a sober clarity and austerity of line and decorations that do not to clash with the monumental marble and colored "scagliola" 16th-17th century altars. One generally enters the church through the little door leading into the left aisle of the church from the "Prato" di Sant'Agostino: it is an excellent vantage point for viewing all the numerous altar-panels painted by great Italian and

ST. CATHERINE'S BIRTHPLACE IN FONTEBRANDA

Back in Via di Città, we turn into the picturesque *Via della Galluzza*, to get to Fontebranda in the territory of the Noble Contrada dell'Oca (Goose). Fontebranda takes its name from the most famous spring in Siena, but is still more renowned throughout the Catholic world because it is the birthplace of Saint Catherine of Siena. Her exalted religious fervor even roused Pope Gregory XI from his torpor. She was born in 1347, probably on 25 March to the dyer Jacopo di Benincasa and to Monna Lapa Piagenti. Catherine's name is especially linked to the history of the papacy, which, at that time, was exiled in Avignon. It was the mystical Sienese Saint who did everything in her power to achieve the return of the popes to Rome (1377). Her famous "Epistles", full of ardent mystical passion, that she addressed, as a Sister in Christ, to popes, princes and rulers throughout Europe brought her literary as well as religious fame. She died in Rome on 29 April 1380 and was canonized by the Sienese pope, Pius II Piccolomini in 1461. She was proclaimed Joint Patron

▼ *Fontebranda and the imposing structure of the Basilica of S. Domenico.*

▲ *Entrance to Saint Catherine's house.*

available for public veneration. Later on, the Confraternity of St. Catherine totally transformed the house into a veritable sanctuary, full of memorabilia and works of art dedicated to the memory of the Saint. The original entrance to the Sanctuary of St. Catherine has always been on the *Vicolo del Tiratoio*. The beautiful Renaissance stone doorway is still visible, and the words "SPONSAE KHRISTI CATERINAE DOMUS" are carved into the lintel. Since the ancient parish church of Sant'Antonio was deliberately demolished in order to build the *Portico dei Comuni d'Italia* (1941), the entrance to St. Catherine's House and its oratories has been through the Portico itself, and every year on the first Sunday of May, consecrated oil is offered by a different Italian municipality. The only old part of the complex is the fine travertine 15th-16th century *well*. Beyond the portico, there is a little loggiaed hallway with slim, elegant columns, generally attributed to Peruzzi. Beyond this hallway, a second *atrium with arches* at the end links the Oratory of the Crucifix with the **Oratory of the Kitchen**, that was partly built in what was probably the Benincasa kitchen. To start with, the room was the

Saint of Rome in 1866 by Pius XII and Joint Patron Saint of Italy in 1939. She was finally proclaimed Doctor of the Church in 1970 by Pope Paul VI. Catherine's probable birthplace was bought for the City of Siena on the 28 January 1466. The inhabitants of Fontebranda demanded that it be permanently

▼ *Wooden statue of St. Catherine by Neroccio di Bartolommeo (Oratory of the Tintoria).*

▲ *The complex of the Portico of the Italian Municipalities.*

◀ *Crucifix known as "of the Stigmata", by a Pisan-Luccan master of the late 12th century.*

▲ *The Keys of Castel Sant'Angelo Given to Pope Urban VI, by Alessandro Casolani.*

▼ *Catherine Giving her Garment to Christ the Pilgrim, by Alessandro Franchi (1896).*

◀ *St Catherine Frees a Possessed Person of the Demon, by Pietro Sorri.*

"Catharinate" Confraternity's prayer room; later, in 1546, it was enlarged by encompassing various smaller rooms, whereupon the resulting enlarged chamber was richly frescoed. The **Church** or **Oratory of the Crucifix** houses the 12th century Pisan school *Crucifix* that, according to tradition, gave St. Catherine her stigmata. Before leaving this mystical place, we need to mention the old **Fountain of Fontebranda**, which is downhill from the Oratory and next to the gateway named after it. It is the most famous and the oldest fountain in Siena and its abundantly flowing waters have quenched the thirst of generations of Sienese, ground the flour of countless mills driven by its flow, and provided a livelihood for tanners and wool-dyers who belonged to the Wool Guild. It was covered with a vaulted roof in 1246. Considerable sums were spent at various intervals to keep the fountain clean and freely flowing, but chiefly to convey to it the waters from the springs which were gradually discovered in other districts, some of them quite distant from Fontebranda. As in all the most important medieval fountains, the first basin was used for drawing drinking water; the second, fed by the overflow from the first, was the drinking trough for cattle and horses, whereas the third was used for laundry.

▲ *Stigmata of St. Catherine, by Bernardino Fungai.*

Fontebranda, today, still has its three solid double, slightly pointed arches, enhanced by the red brick walls and by four stone lions.

Via dei Pittori links the St. Catherine complex to *Via delle Terme* from which one can turn into *Via della Sapienza*, and then, go left, onto **Vicolo della Pallacorda**, one of the most typical medieval alleyways in Siena. The beauty of its somewhat rustic architecture will both surprise and delight the visitor who takes the trouble to make the detour.

◄ *Conversion of Those Condemned to Death, by Lattanzio Bonastri.*

BASILICA OF SAN DOMENICO

Via della Sapienza ends in the piazza of the Basilica of San Domenico, the construction of which, on the little hill called Camporegio, began around 1225, a few years after the founder of the Order, St. Dominic Guzman had been to Siena (1215?) (his visit is not documented, but is almost certain). The land for the church was donated by Fortebraccio Malavolti and the means were partly supplied by the Municipality of Siena and partly given in alms. The Dominican Church and Monastery must have been completed around 1262-65. The church was enlarged, as the fully Gothic style of the nave and of the transept

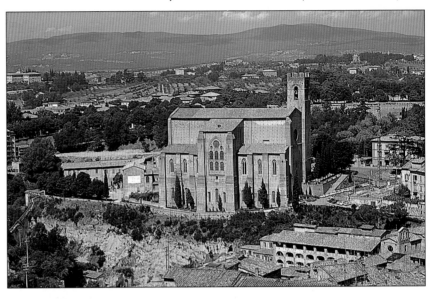

▼ *The Basilica of S. Domenico in the midst of the Sienese countryside.*

◀ *The Basilica of S. Domenico, exterior of the right wing.*

▲ *Via della Sapienza.*

▲ *The interior of the Basilica of S. Domenico.*

▼ *St. Catherine and a follower, by Andrea Vanni* (Chapel of the Vaults).

reveals, towards the middle of the 14th century. The 14th century structure of the basilica is what we can admire today, even if it was disastrously damaged by a fire in 1443, which reduced it to a skeleton and by another in 1531, which started from a chapel and spread to the whole church. A trussed roof covers the vast aisleless nave, built in accordance with the monastic rule of the preaching order, so that the faithful and the preacher should not be separated by any structural obstacle. In 1667, the fresco of *St.* *Catherine and a follower*, unanimously attributed to Andrea Vanni (between 1375 and 1398), was moved to the **Chapel of the Vaults**, which has always been dedicated to the cult of the Sienese saint. Andrea Vanni was a faithful follower of Saint Catherine, who wrote him three letters, so we are moved to believe that the face of the Saint, at least, is the only portrait in existence, painted during her lifetime. Beyond the Chapel of the Vaults, on the right wall of the church, there is a succession of enchanting works of art, such as the *Birth of the Virgin* (1584), one of Alessandro Casolani's most beautiful paintings, justly considered his masterpiece.

The **Chapel of St. Catherine of Siena** was commissioned by Niccolò Bensi in 1460. The head of the Saint, brought here from Rome in 1384, is the central niche in front of the splendid *marble altar*, sculpted in 1469 by Giovanni di Stefano. It is protected by a gilded grille and flanked by two sculpted candle-bearing angels; above the little window, there is a delicate image of the Saint surrounded by cherubim. The chapel walls are completely covered with frescoes and oil painting murals. The decorative work was begun by Sodoma in 1526 who painted the frescoes of the *Mystical Rapture of St. Catherine and the Ecstasy or Eucharistic Vision of the Saint*. They are two world-famous masterpieces by this ardent painter who managed to effect a poetic blend of perfect draftsmanship with a wise use of color, without ever falling into the trap of illustrative languor. Notwithstanding the restricted space at his disposal, the artist managed to impart a solemn grandeur to the monumental figures. Beyond the chapel, against the wall is the *Adoration of the Shepherds*, by Francesco di Giorgio. This painting is of exceptional interest, not only because of its high quality, but also because it is one of few paintings by this great Sienese architect, sculptor and painter. Painted around 1475-80, it no longer shows the influence of Neroccio, but possesses traits that bring it well within the sphere of Verrocchio, with the incisive lines, classical landscape and energetic realism, which we also see in Francesco di Giorgio's beautiful painting of the Nativity (Pinacoteca Nazionale); all these elements link the Sienese painter to the Florentine

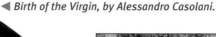

◀ *Birth of the Virgin, by Alessandro Casolani.*

▲ *Tabernacle, by Giovanni di Stefano (Chapel of St. Catherine of Siena).*

◀ *Mystical Ecstasy
of St. Catherine, by Sodoma*
(Chapel of St. Catherine of Siena).

▼ *St. Catherine Liberates
a Woman Possessed (det.),
by Francesco Vanni*
(Chapel of St. Catherine of Siena).

▼ *Birth of Christ, by Francesco di Giorgio Martini.*

▲ *The Madonna and Child Enthroned, Angels and Saints, by Benvenuto di Giovanni.*

▼ *Madonna and Child, by Francesco di Vannuccio: the Almighty and Saints Vincent, Louis, Catherine of Siena and Sebastian, by Sodoma; 15 scenes from the New Testament, 16th cent.*

▲ *St. Barbara Enthroned between Saints Magdalene and Catherine of Alexandria, by Matteo di Giovanni.*

Renaissance at the end of the 15th century, between Verrocchio and Botticelli, when Leonardo's sublime spirit was spreading it wings.

The fifth chapel, where the great *altarpiece* of Guido da Siena used to hang (now in Palazzo Pubblico), at present contains two old Sienese panel paintings; the first shows the *Enthroned Virgin and Child with Angels and Saints Gregory, James, Jerome and Sebastian*, and is one of Benvenuto di Giovanni's best works (1483) with its brilliantly clear gemstone colors that throw the solid, massive figures into relief; the second portrays *St. Barbara enthroned between the Magdalen and St. Catherine of Alexandria*. This recently restored painting is probably Matteo di Giovanni's greatest work (1479); it reveals a supremely luminous quality linked to delicate draftsmanship and a chromatic transparency that the Sienese artist had never before achieved. Matteo also painted the enchanting *Adoration of the Magi* in the lunette above. The left wall of the central nave of the basilica is full of many other works of art, starting from the little painting on the first altar, by Francesco di Vannuccio (c. 1370-80) once attributed to Paolo di Giovanni Fei: it depicts a *Madonna and Child* and is grafted into the center of a much larger painting, by Sodoma, representing the *Almighty, Saints Vincent, Louis, Catherine of Siena and Sebastian*. Below it, above the altar top, runs a predella divided into various orders, with *15 scenes from the New Testament*, that are somewhat reminiscent of Beccafumi or Riccio, by an unknown 16th century Sienese painter.

▶ *Maestà, by Guido da Siena.*

FORTRESS OF SANTA BARBARA

◀ *The fortress of S. Barbara.*

▼ *The Public Gardens of the Lizza and, below, the Enoteca Italica inside the fortress of S. Barbara.*

Leaving San Domenico, and going along Viale dei Mille we reach the site of the former Spanish **fortress** of Don Diego de Mendoza, razed to the ground during a popular uprising in 1552, but then rebuilt a little further south by order of Cosimo I de' Medici after the conquest of Siena in 1555. The Grand Duke personally entrusted one of his architects, Baldassarre Lanci from Urbino, with the construction, in 1561. This powerful defensive and offensive rectangular structure is entirely built in brick and supported on an escarped base, surmounted by a thick bulging brick cordon. There are enormous wedge-shaped bastions on each of the four corners with rounded spurs, surmounted by great *Medici escutcheons*. The extensive and fascinating underground chambers have been transformed into the cellars of the *Enoteca Italica*, which is famous for its Italian wine tasting.

The **public gardens of the Lizza,** opposite the Medici fortress, were laid out in the 19th century.

PORTA CAMOLLIA

From the Lizza gardens we take Via Montanini and then Via di Camollia to reach Porta di Camollia, the strongest and most dreaded gateway of Siena opened onto and concluded the Via Cassia, that came from Florence. The gateway we see today was rebuilt in 1604, to designs by Alessandro Casolani. According to historical sources, the stone decorations were carved by the sculptor Domenico Cafaggi. The external arch of Porta Camollia bears the famous inscription that was carved onto it to honor Ferdinand I de' Medici's arrival in Siena: COR MAGIS TIBI SENA PANDIT (Siena welcomes you with open arms) and that is now symbolic of the city's hospitality. Outside the Porta Camollia, we come to the Villa Seminario Regionale of Montarioso, that housed the **Museo Diocesano di Arte Sacra** (The Diocesan Museum of Sacred Art) of great historical and artistic interest. The museum is temporarily closed and will eventually be moved to the Ospedale di Santa Maria della Scala. One of the most outstanding pieces in the museum is the *Nursing Madonna (Madonna del Latte)* by A. Lorenzetti.

◀ *Porta Camollia.*

▲ *Nursing Madonna (Madonna del Latte),*
by Ambrogio Lorenzetti
(Museo Diocesano di Arte Sacra).

Piazza dei Salimbeni

Returning to Via di Camollia and Via Montanini, we come to Piazza Salimbeni. The piazza, as we see it today, was redesigned at the end of the XIX century by the purist architect Giuseppe Partini. Most of it, on the right side, was taken from the gardens of the Palazzo Spannocchi. The front was a long corridor with the **Palazzo della Dogana, Palazzo Tantucci** and finally the **Rocca dei Salimbeni** on the left.

▼ *The Rocca dei Salimbeni, headquarters of the Monte dei Paschi di Siena, with the nineteenth century façade by Partini.*

▲ *Piazza Salimbeni with the monument to Sallustio Bandini; Palazzo Tantucci on the left; the headquarters of the Monte dei Paschi di Siena in the background and, on the right, the façade of Palazzo Spannocchi, by Partini (1881).*

▲ *The new staircase of the Rocca by the architect Spadolini (Palazzo Salimbeni, headquarters of the Monte dei Paschi di Siena).*

▼ *The Madonna of Mercy,
by Benvenuto di Giovanni;
the saints are attributed to Fungai*
(Collection of the Monte
dei Paschi di Siena).

The rocca, or keep was one of the major fortified complexes of medieval Siena. After the uprisings of 1264 and 1268 the keep was torn down and later rebuilt, but the Republic finally banished the Salimbeni family and confiscated their property in 1419. It was taken over the by city which established the salt and grain tax offices there. After it was purchased by the Monte dei Paschi di Siena bank in 1866 for the sum of Lit. 60,743 the architect Giuseppe Partini was commissioned to remodel it. In the spirit of Gothic revival that was then in vogue he made extensive changes to what remained of the original structure, raising and adding new structures and wings in imitation Gothic style. *The monument to Sallustio Bandini* (1880) by Tito Sarocchi was then placed in the middle of the square. The current headquarters of the **Monte dei Paschi di Siena**,

◀ *Orestes Killing Aegisthus
and Clytemnestra, by Bernardino Mei*
(Collection of the Monte
dei Paschi di Siena).

◀ *The Ailing Antiochus,
by Bernardino Mei*
(Collection of the Monte
dei Paschi di Siena).

▼ *Pietà, by the Maestro
dell'Osservanza*
(Collection of the Monte
dei Paschi di Siena).

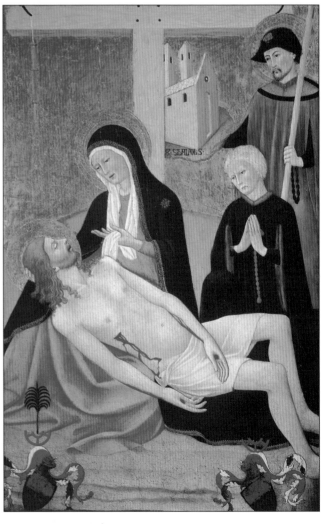

◀ *The Madonna of the Vetturini, by Giovanni di Paolo*
(Collection of the Monte dei Paschi di Siena).

◄ *Jerome Comforted by the Angels,*
by Rutilio Manetti (Collection
of the Monte dei Paschi di Siena).

restored by the architect Pier Luigi Spadolini (1962-73) who succeeded in gracefully combining modern structures with the old walls, consists of the following 13th century architectural elements: the *tower,* the *Fondaco dei Salimbeni,* the *Rocca,* and the *Palazzetto di Ranieri Salimbeni.* Along with the historic archives that contain much information about the economic history of Siena, the Rocca dei Salimbeni also contains many extremely valuable artworks that the bank has collected over the years. It is thanks to the Monte dei Paschi di Siena that many masterpieces that had been scattered throughout Italy over the past three centuries are now being brought back to Siena, where they were created during the era of the Republic. The collection includes works by Pietro Lorenzetti, Sassetta, Givoanni di Paolo, Sano di Pietro, Beccafumi and many others.

▼ *Stories of the Chaste Susanna,*
by Francesco Vanni (Collection
of the Monte dei Paschi di Siena).

▲ *Palazzo Tolomei.*

Piazza dei Tolomei

From Piazza Salimbeni, we take Via Banchi di Sopra to Piazza dei Tolomei. In the middle of the square there is a column, surmounted by the *Sienese she-wolf,* by Domenico Arrighetti, called the "Cavedone" (1610). The piazza is named after the famous Sienese family, the most powerful after the Salimbeni, their longtime rivals for domination over the city; the Tolomei also disputed and claimed supremacy over the government itself. The piazza is dominated by the **Palazzo dei Tolomei**, that came into being after the Castellare of the Consorteria dei Tolomei (which in 1290 included some 120 families) was demolished.

Notwithstanding the disastrous fire of 1277, the splendid building we see today is certainly one of the finest in Siena, and probably dates back to 1270, with its elegant, double mullioned windows and the great hall on the ground floor which was restructured between 1430 and 1444. Today it is headquarters of the Sienese branch of the **Cassa di Risparmio di Firenze**, and a number

▲ *The small cloister of S. Cristoforo.*

▼ *The church of S. Cristoforo.*

of sculptured fragments (*small capitals, lion-heads, the torso of a she-wolf*), that were found during the 1971 restoration works, are also displayed here. On the opposite side of the square is the **Church of San Cristoforo**, one of the oldest in Siena (11th-12th century), famed for having been the headquarters of the Greater Council of the Republic (Consiglio della Campana) in the 12th and 13th centuries. Unfortunately, after the terrible 1798 earthquake, the church was shortened and was given its neoclassical façade, by Tommaso and Francesco Paccagnini (1800), with the two (1802) *statues* by Giuseppe Silini and the Tolomei *coat of arms*. Next to the church is a charming *little cloister*, probably built around the beginning of the 13th century, with brick columns and stone capitals, that was rebuilt to a large extent during the restorations done in 1921.

BASILICA OF SAN FRANCESCO

Behind the church of San Cristoforo, along Via del Giglio, we come to Piazza San Francesco and the Church of San Francesco. Anonymous Sienese chroniclers mention 1228 as the year in which the first church dedicated to St. Francis was built on the hill of the Castellaccia di Ovile.

▲ *Apse of S. Francesco.*

▼ *Neogothic façade of the Basilica of S. Francesco.*

▼ *Portal of 1400, by Francesco di Giorgio Martini.*

The decoration of the rough stone façade (the neo-Gothic decorations we see today were done in the late 19th century) with black and white marble stripes was started just before the end of the 13th century, interrupted after only half the façade had been covered and never completed. The church, on the other hand, was enlarged, because it was too small, in 1326. Only the façade and the right side of the old Romanesque church remain; the left side was demolished once the new left wall had been completed and joined to the roof. The presbytery was entirely reconstructed on pow-

▲ *Cloister of S. Francesco.*

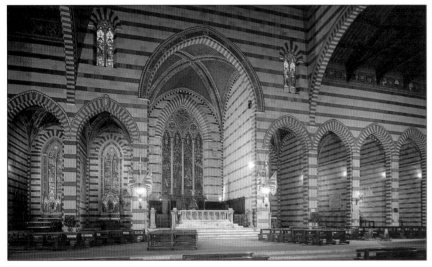

▲ *The transept of the Basilica of S. Francesco.*

▼ *Crucifixion, by Pietro Lorenzetti.*

erful arches, that open onto a magnificent underground crypt built into the steep hillside. The new enlarged church was finished in 1475, but then, in 1482, the walls were raised to match the increased width of the renovated church. Francesco di Giorgio was almost certainly the architect entrusted with the latter project. The lovely main portal, in pure Sienese Renaissance style, is also worthy of his hand. After the

▲ *St. Louis of Toulouse Taking His Leave from Pope Boniface VIII,* by Ambrogio Lorenzetti.

▼ *Fresco in the form of a polyptych, by Lippo Vanni.*

façade was remodeled, the portal was moved inside the basilica, against the left wall where we can admire it today. The structural parts of the church that we see today were built by Francesco di Giorgio, but nearly all the treasures it used to contain were destroyed by the terrible fire of 25 August 1655, that even burned the marble and the altar. The few surviving paintings are now in the Pinacoteca Nazionale of Siena. In the (eighth) Bandini Piccolomini Chapel (dedicated to St. Bernardino), there are two great frescoes by Ambrogio Lorenzetti, portraying the *Martyrdom of Franciscan Friars* and *St. Louis of Toulouse taking his leave from Pope Boniface VIII after abdicating his claim to the throne in favor of his brother Robert d'Anjou.* Notwithstanding their poor state of conservation, the frescoes still reveal Ambrogio's inventiveness and realism.

BASILICA OF SANTA MARIA DI PROVENZANO

Returning from Piazza San Francesco along Via delle Vergini, we reach the Basilica of Santa Maria di Provenzano, in honor of whose much venerated image the Palio race of 2 July is run. The Standard (Palio) is brought to the church before the race. On 2 July, it is taken to the Piazza del Campo and given to the winning Contrada, then, amidst a turmoil of rejoicing members of the victorious Contrada and of the allied or friendly Contrade, it is taken back to the Basilica, if only for a few minutes, to offer solemn thanks to the Virgin of Provenzano for the victory.

Construction of the basilica was started in 1595, and, architecturally speaking, was completed in 1604. It was consecrated on 16 October

▲ *Mass of St. Cerbone, by Rutilio Manetti.*

1611. The design is based on the Roman church of Gesù, by Vignola, that best reflects the spirit of the Counter Reformation: a single, shortened nave, to facilitate preaching and a series of side altars, which, in this church, are simply set against the side walls and not surrounded by separate chapels as they are in the Roman church.

◀ *The collegiate church of S. Maria in Provenzano.*

PALAZZO PICCOLOMINI

Proceeding towards Via Banchi di Sotto, we cross one of the most fascinating medieval districts of Siena, which was where the great *castellari*, fortified mansions, used to stand. Next to the castellare of the Uguccioni family is the seat of the *University of Siena*, and facing it, the grandiose Palazzo Piccolomini, that houses the *State Archives*. It was begun around the middle of the 15th century, by Bernardo Gambarelli, known as Rossellino, who brought the purest Florentine Re-

▼ *The entrance to the Castellare of the Ugurgieri.*

▲ *The façade of Palazzo Piccolomini in Via Banchi di Sotto, now home to the State Archives.*

naissance civil architecture to Siena. Rossellino was the architect Pius II Piccolomini commissioned to build his model Renaissance jewel town of Pienza. The State Archives of Siena contain the famous and unique collection known as the **Museo delle tavolette della Biccherna**, that comprises 103 panel paintings and only two painted canvases, originally the covers of the Biccherna and Municipal Tax registers (Gabella del Comune), as well as those of the Ospedale di

Santa Maria della Scala and other Sienese administrative archives. Towards the middle of the 13th century the Biccherna (the main financial magistrature of Siena) adopted the practice of having the covers of the most important registers in its offices painted. The practice was also adopted by other financial magistratures and continued up to the 18th century. The Biccherna collection constitutes a marvelously complete pictorial history of four centuries of Sienese life.

▼ *The Victory of Camollia (after 1526), Gabella panel, by Giovanni di Lorenzo Cini (State Archives, Museo delle Biccherne).*

◀ *Siena "al tenpo dei Tremuoti", Biccherna panel of the year 1467, by Francesco di Giorgio Martini (State Archives, Museo delle Biccherne).*

▲ *Annunciation with saints, Gabella panel by a Sienese artist (July/Dec. 1456) (State Archives, Museo delle Biccherne).*

◀ *The finances of the Commune in times of peace and in times of war, Biccherna panel of the year 1468, by Benvenuto di Giovanni (State Archives, Museo delle Biccherne).*

SYNAGOGUE

The Jewish Temple of Siena, in the University district, was built in 1756, to neoclassical designs by the architect Giuseppe del Rosso. The wooden decorations were made by two master carpenters: Niccolò Ianda and Pietro Rossi. The *columns* flanking the Ark are supposed to have been made out of pieces of marble that came from Jerusalem and are particularly worthy of note.

One of the finest surviving pieces of the original rich furnishing is the *circumcision throne* which was made in 1860. The Temple follows the Sephardic rite. Six curiously fashioned marble cavities have been recently discovered in the entrance hall. They are dated 1600 and were used for collecting offerings and contributions for the Jewish community of the time.

▲ *Entrance to the synagogue.*

◀ *Interior of the synagogue.*

by Antonio Zazzeroni

The Contrade (Districts) of Siena were created between the end of the 12th and the beginning of the 13th century, and were responsible for administrative matters (tax collection, road maintenance) and public safety (police), etc. These institutions, that were based in the parish churches which served both for public meetings and worship, were governed by a kind of mayor who was answerable directly to the Podestà (Chief of Justice) and was assisted by councilors elected by the people of the Contrada. The structure of the Contrade was completed after the formation of Compagnie Militari (the army of the Republic) in which every able man from 18 to 70 years of age had to serve. The Compagnie Militari were, in turn, grouped into the so-called "Terzi" (Thirds), corresponding to the three territorial divisions or districts of the city: the Terzo di Città (a white cross on red ground), the Terzo di San Martino (St. Martin and the beggar on a burgundy ground), and the Terzo di Camollia (a black K on white ground). Each Terzo was commanded by a Gonfaloniere Maestro, or standard-bearer. The Captain of the People bore a standard with a Crowned Lion Rampant on red ground: he was the supreme Commander of the Militia. In the 14th century, the clans of Siena were distributed among the 42 Contrade, which were reduced to 23 between the 15th and 16th centuries. In time, the political and administrative reasons that had led to the creation of the Contrade virtually disappeared and the latter turned their attention more and more to the organization of public games that long flourished in the town. The 23 Contrade took the names of *Aquila* (Eagle), *Bruco* (Caterpillar), *Chiocciola* (Snail), *Civetta* (Owl), *Drago* (Dragon), *Gallo* (Rooster), *Giraffa* (Giraffe), *Istrice* (Porcupine), *Leone* (Lion), *Liocomo or Leocorno* (Unicorn), *Liofante or Torre* (Elefant or Tower), *Lupa* (She-wolf), *Montone* (Ram), *Nicchio* (Shell), *Oca* (Goose), *Onda* (Wave), *Orso* (Bear), *Pantera* (Panther), *Quercia* (Oak), *Selvalta or Selva* (Forest), *Spadaforte* (Sword), *Tartuca* (Tortoise), and *Vipera* (Viper). No documentation exists explaining why the names (that were probably the fruit of popular imagination or related to some special event) were actually chosen. 1675 seems to be when six of these Contrade were suppressed, to wit: Gallo, Leone, Orso, Quercia, Spadaforte and Vipera.

◀ *"Palio" of 1719.*

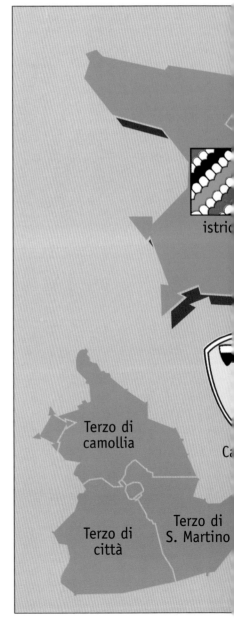

THE CONTRADE
TODAY

Today's Contrade are old institutions with a following that keeps growing year after year. The members are committed, insofar as possible, to carrying on their traditions and supporting them financially. (Each contradaiolo -contrada member- pays annual dues, called "protettorato") The organization of the contrade consists of decision-making and executive bodies that are established as needed. One of the most important sectors is dedicated to the young people who are the future of the contrade and the Palio. They are taught the history of the race, with specific emphasis on their respective contrade. The "Women's group" of each contrada generally deals with this issue almost exclusively. The women's group is also in charge of preparing parties for the little ones, on the feast of the Nativity of the Virgin, 8 September. The children decorate the shrine with the image of the Virgin Mary in the most typical part of the district and in the evening a street dinner is held just for them. The most solemn event, however, is the feast day of the patron saint of the contrada which is celebrated on the Sunday closest to the day. The streets are illuminated by the "braccialetti", carved wooden lamps, painted in the contrada's colors, holding bunches of light-bulbs and with old terra-cotta lamps filled with tallow and wick that burn through most of the night. On the eve of the feast, the Prior of the Contrada, accompanied by the Seggio (the governing body) and the Popolo (the people of the contrada) goes to the boundary of the district and meets the leaders

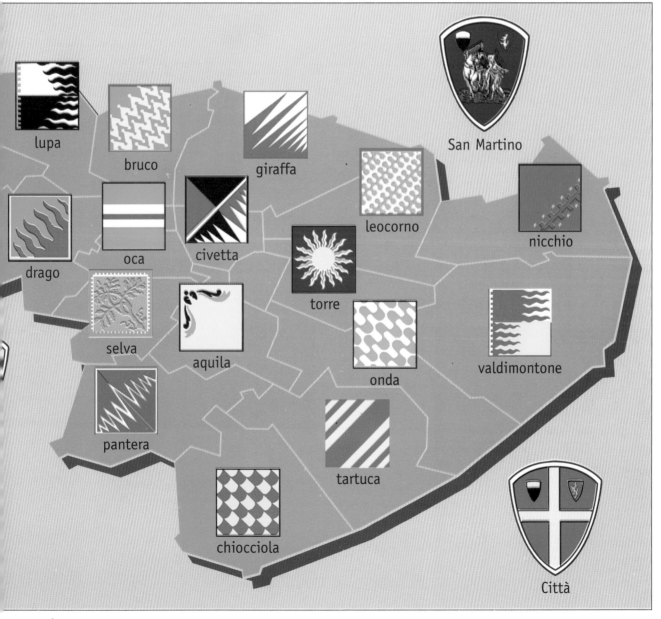

AQUILA
(EAGLE)

BRUCO
(CATERPILLAR)

CHIOCCIOLA
(SNAIL)

CIVETTA
(OWL)

DRAGO
(DRAGON)

GIRAFFA
(GIRAFFE)

ISTRICE
(PORCUPINE)

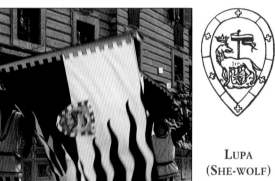

LEOCORNO
(UNICORN)

LUPA
(SHE-WOLF)

NICCHIO
(SHELL)

OCA
(GOOSE)

ONDA
(WAVE)

PANTERA
(PANTHER)

SELVA
(FOREST)

TARTUCA
(TORTOISE)

TORRE
(TOWER)

VALDIMONTONE
(RAM)

▲ *Drummers, trumpeters and standard-bearers at the beginning of the historical procession.*

of the allied contrade. Then, preceded by drums and standard-bearers they go to the oratory for Vespers. At the end of the service the people pour back into the streets for the "children's palio", the "sack race", the "climbing the May-pole" and other games invented for the occasion. But, above all, they sing a song, that is common to all seventeen contrade; it is about Siena and is embellished with extemporaneous rhymes either singing the praises of the contrada or ridiculing its rivals. Naturally, wine is served in abundance and the celebrations last late into the night. In the morning Mass is celebrated in the Oratory and the "Comparsa", consisting of dozens of participants, including drummers and standard-bearers, winds its way through the city to pay tribute to the "protectors". The procession is repeated the following Sunday through streets outside the city walls, and is known as the "giro di campagna" or "country tour". In the evening the procession returns to the city, followed by the Prior, the Seggio and the Popolo.

THE SOCIETÀ DI CONTRADA

The "Società di Contrada" were established early in the 19th century to organize the contrada's yearly activities. These associations, with headquarters in premises adjacent to those of the contrada itself and that include rooms for meetings, dances and entertainment, game rooms, refreshment bar and a well-equipped kitchen are involved in many cultural, athletic and social-charity (such as the blood donors group) activities and programs. The bar and other services are managed by the contradaioli, who without pay or social distinctions take turns serving at the bar or waiting on tables. The kitchens are run mainly by the women's group that prepares the dinners and the banquet on the eve of the Palio (if the contrada is running that season), known as the Cena della Prova Generale, or Dress Rehearsal Dinner, for 1,000 or more guests.

"DRAWING" THE CONTRADE

The first act of the Palio is the drawing: it is held about one month before the race (the last Sunday in May for the July palio and the Sunday after the July race for the August palio). Ten contrade take part in the Carriera or race. The rules governing the drawing are actually much less complex than they seem at first glance. The July race is run by the seven contrade that did not participate in the preceding July edition, and the other

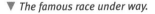
▼ *The famous race under way.*

three are chosen, by lot, from amongst the contrade that had participated, thus giving each edition of the race the required 10 participating contrade. The same method is applied to the Palio held in August. Thus, the two "carriere", July and August are completely independent of each other insofar as the participating contrade are concerned. It may happen that a particularly lucky Contrada gets to participate in both races in one year, but that means that it will be automatically excluded from the races the following year, unless its name is drawn again. On the morning of the day of the drawing, the banners of the seven contrade that are participating by right are displayed on the first floor windows of the Palazzo Pubblico. In the afternoon, the other three participating contrade are drawn by lot; this is done by the mayor and the Captains. The flags of the three selected contrade are then displayed to tell the crowds, anxiously gathered outside the building which have been selected. The flags of the contrade that were not chosen are displayed from the upper floor, telling which ones will be automatically allowed to run in the following years' race. In the event of an extraordinary palio held for some special event, all ten contrade may run.

PREPARING THE PIAZZA DEL CAMPO

For a Sienese, the words "Terra in Piazza", literally earth on the Piazza del Campo, mean Palio: joy, hope and rivalry. The whole town is transformed and pulses with intense, unforgettable, almost magical life, especially if you have the opportunity to watch from the top of some tower in the evening. Shouts, laughter, and songs surge from street to street, from square to square, up to the final explosion (this time, only in the winning contrada) after the race. These are the moments of great joy to a Sienese, and can only be compared to the moment in which the Palio is handed down to the winning Contrada in the Piazza and to the other moment of totally pagan exultation that assails the people of the victorious Contrada when they pour into Santa Maria di Provenzano or into the Cathedral to offer thanksgiving for their victory. Several days before the race, the road around the Piazza is covered with a thick layer of earth, to make it easier for the horses to run. The stands for the spectators, the Judges' stand, where the Captains and Lieutenants of the Contrade also sit, as well as the stand of the Priori are set up against the buildings around the square. The former near the Costarella dei Barbieri (the start and finish line), the latter near the Chiasso Largo. The concave center of the square, capable of holding some 40,000 spectators, is surrounded with metal barriers. At the Costarella dei Barbieri, a contraption, known as the "verrocchio" is set up. The "mossiere", the official and only starter uses this device that causes a thick rope, known as the "canapo" that has been drawn taut across the track by a winch behind the barriers, to drop. A few meters behind this rope there is a shorter and thinner one stretched between the stands and the winch leaving just enough room for the horses to fit between the two ropes for the start of the race. A metal cage containing firecrackers that are set off at various moments during the race as signals is hoisted up next to the winch.

◀ *An impressive picture of Piazza del Campo during the Palio.*

THE "TRATTA" (SELECTING THE HORSES)

Four days before the Palio (on 29 June for the July Palio and on 13 August for the Palio of the Assumption), the owners of the horses, (who must have veterinary certificates) lead their horses into the Podestà courtyard of the Palazzo Pubblico, early in the morning. The municipal officials identify the horses with a number called the "coscia" (flank) number, according to the order in which they are presented. A veterinarian, appointed by the City Council, checks the medical certificates and the horses' health. The horses are taken out, in groups of five or six at a time, ridden by the owners' jockeys or jockeys who ran in the Palio the year before. The horses have to circle the track three times (about 1000 meters in all). After the trials, three veterinarians very carefully check each horse and the Captains of the Contrade running in the Palio choose the ten horses that will run in the Palio. In the meantime, a large number of "contradaioli" usually gather in front of Palazzo Pubblico to watch the public assignment of the horses. The Mayor and the 10 Contrade Captains sit on a dais, set up in front of the Palazzo Public; there are also two urns on the dais. The 10 selected horses are led into horse boxes situated on the left of the platform. The Mayor puts 10 numbers (from 1 to 10) into one urn and the names of the 10 Contrade in the other. Two signboards hung above the dais, on the façade of the Palazzo Pubblico, will show which horse has been allotted to which Contrada. No substitutions are allowed after this time, if a horse falls sick or even dies before the race, the Contrada cannot replace its assigned steed. The "barbareschi" (grooms) who will lovingly care for their Contrada's horse up to the start of

▲ The cart (Carroccio) with the "Palio".

the race, wearing the colors of their respective Contrada, each take charge of the assigned horse, and lead it to the Contrada's stable.

THE TRIALS, THE PARTIES AND THE PALIO

As from the afternoon of the day of the "Tratta" the "barberi" (steeds) are taken for practice runs six times (morning and afternoon) before the race. They are ridden by the jockeys who are selected by the Contrade on the basis of the skill, experience and weight. The Captains and their Lieutenants spend these days getting the "partiti" (parties/allies) together, to scheme on how to damage the rival Contrade and above all how to win the race, and they are not above using bribery. The negotiations continue in absolute secrecy right up to the last moment before the Palio. At last the day of days dawns. Early in the morning, the Archbishop of Siena celebrates Jockeys' Mass in the Cappella di Piazza, and the last trial, called the "provaccia" is run shortly afterwards. Then, the jockeys who will participate in the Palio are officially registered by the City Council. In the early afternoon, each Contrada church is crammed full of contrada members, while the co-rector blesses both horse and jockey and then, breaks the silence with the ritual words, "Go, and return victorious!". The "Comparse" of the Contrada, wearing their· splendid costumes and waving their banners, start off for Piazza del Duomo, where the historical pageant forms up in front of the Prefecture. It also includes the representatives of the Sienese City Council, of the "guilds", of the University, of the City Councils of Massa Marittima and Montalcino, that took part in important events in Siena's history. Last of all comes the "Carroccio" the standard bearing cart, drawn by oxen and followed by a trumpeters and a mounted escort of knights from the noble Sienese families. The cart carries the "Balzana", Sienese Standard, and the Palio: a silk banner painted by famous Italian and foreign artists (traditionally the Palio for the July race is by a Sienese artist, while a famous artist from outside Siena creates the banner for the August race. The Palio, is given to the winning Contrada,

whereas the Contrada judged the best during the procession, both because of the stateliness of the Comparsa's behavior, as well as for the skills of the drummer and flag-wavers, will subsequently receive the *masgalano*, a finely chased silver plate. After accompanying their Comparsa to Piazza del Duomo, the people of the contrade take up their positions in piazza del Campo. Once the historical pageant has gone around the earth track on the Piazza del Campo, all the costumed representatives of the Contrade take their seats on the stand set up in front of the Palazzo Public. One drummer and one standard bearer for each Contrada stay on the track for final standard display, which is the last salute paid to the crowd before the race; in the meantime the Palio is hoisted into position on the Judges' Stand. And the race is on! At the signal, the horses, which are ridden bare-back by the jockeys, wearing the colors of the contrade and hard metal caps called "zucchini", are led out of the Courtyard of the Podestà. As they emerge, each jockey is given a "nerbo" or crop (made out of a dried bull's phallus) that can be used to urge on their own horses, or to hit the opposing horses or jockeys. They proceed to the "mossa", starting post where a special machine draws lots as to the order in which the horses are to en-

ter the gap between the two ropes. As soon as the horse of the tenth and last Contrada enters the gap, the "mossiere" (starter) gives the signal which will be repeated if he judges that the horses have gotten off to a false start. As soon as the rope drops, the horses spurt forward and the jockeys fight each other in every way they can. One of the horses will be the winner, even if he gets to the finish riderless, because it is the horse that gets to the end of the race that wins, not the rider. The deliriously exultant contrada members brandish their banners as the Palio is handed down to them from the judges' stand and chant their way towards the Victory Banquet. And the night will resound to their songs of joy. Torches will burn brightly from the Mangia tower, while the colors of the winning contrada hang triumphantly outside the triple mullioned window of the Palace.

THE VICTORIOUS CONTRADA CELEBRATES THE PALIO

The Contrade that have won the two Palio races of the year generally organize two great banquets, a few days apart, in the month of September. The contrada is decked with flags and lights and trestle tables are set up along the streets, for the some 3-4000 hungry participants at the Victory Banquet. The Prior of the Contrada, flanked by the Captain and the victorious jockey will be given the places of honor, together with the officials and specially invited guests. Most important of all, in the center, opposite the places of honor, a small paddock with a manger, will be set up for the real winner, the horse. A journal entitled *Numero Unico* published by the contrada recounts the story of the race and its protagonists through pictures and articles.

▼ The "Victory Banquet" in Piazza Jacopo della Quercia (contrada dell'Aquila).

INDEX